Hutong Heartthrobs

TAMMY TREICHEL

EARNSHAW BOOKS

Hutong Heartthrobs

By Tammy Treichel

Trade Paper: 978-988-8843-74-9
Digital: 978-988-8904-00-6

© 2024 Tammy Treichel

BIOGRAPHY & AUTOBIOGRAPHY

Tamara (Tammy) and Jackie in their Beijing neighborhood of Yonghegong/Guozijian
Photo credits: 李科伟 (Li Kewei), 潘雪 (Pan Xue), Daniel K. Schweitzer

EB216

All rights reserved. No part of this book may be reproduced in material form, by any means, whether graphic, electronic, mechanical or other, including photocopying or information storage, in whole or in part. May not be used to prepare other publications without written permission from the publisher except in the case of brief quotations embodied in critical articles or reviews. For information contact info@earnshawbooks.com

Published in Hong Kong by Earnshaw Books Ltd.

For more understanding, friendship and, yes, love between China and the West!

For my father, Horst Treichel (1939-2015), who (occasionally) had an open mind. For Gerd. And for my Uncle Siegfried (1932-2022), who together with his wife Jutta believed in "global families."

新春快乐

PREFACE

Who would have thought a US academic and a Chinese migrant worker-turned-movie actor would find true love in a Beijing hutong?

Well, it happened.

I had been itching to write a book about my China adventures for some time, a manageable memoir that wouldn't turn out to be a Herculean task, and it was on my mother's birthday, May 19, 2018, that I sat down with my Chinese life partner, Jackie, a migrant worker and security guard-turned-actor, and made a start.

My American mother, Joan Arehart-Treichel, who is a successful science writer, said it would be challenging to integrate my experiences with Jackie's—two people from completely different cultures with different mother tongues. But I had no doubts. I gathered all my previous journal entries, writings and professional translations of media reports about Jackie and started hammering away. My mother was very encouraging (she published her fifth book at age eighty, titled *Warding Off Evildoers*).

Jackie jotted down his memories in Chinese at the kitchen table in our Beijing hutong house and sat with me at the computer dictating them, correcting as we went along. It was a labor of love.

There are other, sad Chinese love stories and movies about migrant workers, like the famous TV series *Beijing Love Story* in which Jackie played an extra in the suicide attempt scene. But Jackie and I have our own Beijing love story with a totally different plot. Ours is ongoing and upbeat.

It is not only about my love for Jackie, a migrant worker and jack-of-all-trades, and his love for me, but about our love for a certain city in China, Beijing, and a certain way of life in its narrow meandering streets called hutongs and the houses there, often made of mud and stone, others of elegantly carved and painted wood, perfectly chiselled stone and furnished with refinement. Ours was the former, made of mud and stone, with its own charms, quirks and a Venus de Milo under a bell jar on the fridge.

In August 2018, I lectured new recruits at the media organization where I was an editor, and the question-and-answer session was vigorous. A young, rather proactive Chinese man stood up, clutched the microphone and surprised me.

"Thank you for your lecture. I have no questions about it, but I want to know about YOU. Why did you come to China? When did you come? What are your impressions?" he asked.

I had been asked similar questions before. These vindicated my belief that maybe a book about my life in Beijing, especially one entwined with Jackie's, might be of interest to both Chinese and foreign readers.

This book attempts to bridge or narrow the cultural and social divide between people from totally different backgrounds: a rather stubborn American woman with a PhD in American literature and a country boy, migrant worker, security guard, jack-of-all trades-turned-movie actor (and Jackie Chan's stand-in) who share a sense of adventure. Both came to China's capital to pursue their dreams.

Some of the facts in here are somewhat colored by my imagination. Where necessary, I have taken artistic liberties in reconstructing dialogue when journal entries were insufficient and condensed episodes for the sake of flow. But writing

TAMMY TREICHEL

these experiences down allowed me to reflect on myself, my relationship with Jackie and get to know special things about him, and by extension, China — things I wouldn't have learned otherwise.

1

WHAT ARE THE ODDS?

Life is all about doors and windows.

People often ask me: "How did you meet Jackie, your Chinese better half?" It was on May 9, 2012, a typical May day in Beijing—the poplar leaves had turned a lush green, the sky was blue, and the sun was shining. The air was pretty fresh, too. There was a sense of languor, mystique and hope in the air, hope for more sunny days and adventure ahead, that strange mix that May brings.

It was early afternoon, and I was taking the subway after

working the morning shift at my workplace. I traveled more than one hour to and from work and changed lines twice—from downtown Beijing on Lines 2, 13 and 15, to Wangjing (望京), where I lived.

I enjoyed the subway because it was reliable, clean and convenient compared with the subways I was used to in Washington, D.C., my hometown, and in New York and San Francisco; it was new and pretty much spotless.

There were the microphone-lugging singers and guitar players trying to make some extra money. Nowadays, however, there are "safety stewards" on some lines to ensure the cars are free of "unsolicited entertainment."

Migrant workers hauled huge bundles and then used them as couches, elderly men read newspapers moving their lips, young people played games on digital devices that looked like Game Boys. This was the cusp of the digital age; today, commuters stare mainly at their smart phones.

Cartoons on the TV screens of the Beijing subway provided silent entertainment, and before the advent of smart phones, many passengers would stare zombie-like at them. Some of the little movies were instructional, teaching Line 2 passengers the importance of safety and hygiene—a man ran away from a fiendishly personified pillar of smoke and filth grinning wickedly; elsewhere an elderly lady conscientiously washed a wound on her finger. And there were news briefs, cooking demos and fashion shows.

I remembered when I was offered a job as an English-language editor at a local news organization in 2009. The interviewer appeared to think Beijing and I would be a match.

"You will like Beijing," he predicted. "The subway is good and so is the food."

Little did he know that his words would prove to be prophetic.

And that there would be more to love than just the subway and the food. A Chinese friend told me, "China can be a fantastic place for foreigners."

Fast forward to 2012. In Wangjing West (望京西) on Line 13, I entered a subway car to the next stop, Wangjing, on Line 15. I wasn't expecting anything special. I just stood there, with my purse slung over my right shoulder and my tote bag on a rail next to the window. I drowsily gazed into the reflection as the train was speeding through the dim tunnel.

Suddenly, I noticed a huge smiley face in the reflection of the subway car window. What was that?

I spun around.

A handsome young Chinese man with a rather big head was standing before me. He had chocolate brown eyes and bow-shaped lips and was now smiling a little shyly. When I first set eyes on Jackie, it was not unlike Romeo and Juliet eyeing each other through the glass of a fish tank in the movie *Romeo + Juliet* (1996) starring Leonardo DiCaprio and Claire Danes. However, our encounter had a comedic touch and this conversation and the ensuing ones between us were in Chinese, although during our first encounter, he might have used one or two English sentences as an opener.

"Do you speak Chinese?" the young stranger asked, looking at me rather intensely.

"A little, but my Chinese isn't that good," I replied, casting my eyes down.

"Where are you from?" he asked.

"I am American, my name is Tammy," I answered, giving my nickname as it was easier for most Chinese and foreigners than the more formal "Tamara," which unfortunately sounds a bit like a Chinese cuss word involving mothers.

"My name is Jackie," my new acquaintance said, with a

winning smile.

When I got off at Wangjing station, he got off as well, and we continued to talk. I noticed he liked to look into my eyes for a while before shyly averting his gaze.

As we were walking through the station, Jackie took out a portable device for watching little videos and he showed me a segment from the movie *Forrest Gump*, in English with Chinese subtitles. Forrest Gump's mother, on her deathbed, tells her son, "Life is a box of chocolates. You never know what you are going to get."

Was this a classic pick-up line in China? I wondered. Was I a piece of chocolate? I thought the *Forrest Gump* quote was a funny but also true observation about life. I laughed.

This reminded me of my little performance for a New Year's party at my workplace; I was pounding a tambourine and two foreign coworkers were playing guitars. The Chinese MC introduced our band and later, he asked, "So, what do you think about China?"

"Well," I said matter-of-factly, clutching my tambourine, "China is like a box of chocolates — you never know what you are going to get." That well-known line resonated with the Chinese audience as *Forrest Gump* was popular in China.

"How romantic!" the MC said and then went on to other things.

Back to Jackie and me. Of course, it was not love at first sight as it takes time to truly develop feelings. But it definitely was curiosity and intrigue at first sight!

I had nothing planned for the remainder of that afternoon nor had Jackie, so we sat down on a bench and chatted in a little park surrounded by high-rises near the subway station. A large stone near us bore the ancient carved Chinese character for "home" (家).

Jackie was very theatrical, his eyes glowed, and he had nice pearly teeth and crow's feet when he smiled. I thought the crow's feet made his eyes look expressive, maybe he had developed them from smiling so much. When I pointed them out, however, he didn't seem too pleased; maybe he thought they made him look old.

He pointed out my back was not straight, and that I should be careful not to slouch, because I didn't want a bent back when I was an old woman. So Jackie offered me his first piece of advice: take better care of myself and sleep on a hard bed, as Chinese tend to do.

He held up his arm to the sunlight and I held up mine, and we laughed when we noticed we had the same skin color — his skin was white for a Chinese person, while my arms were tanned, despite my having adopted the habit of Chinese ladies of carrying a parasol. Pale complexions are still treasured in China and a sign that someone doesn't have to toil in the sun.

I felt very relaxed and natural talking to Jackie. He told me he also lived in the Wangjing neighborhood, in a sublet one-bedroom apartment shared with five other people. He paid 15 yuan (about USD 2) per night, unless he slept elsewhere.

He sometimes ate outside at a little shop offering noodles, tomatoes and eggs, thousand-year-old (or preserved) eggs, cucumbers, salted peanuts and beer. Later we would have a meal there, sitting on rickety stools. Close by was also a tailor's where he had his clothes dry-cleaned — I would discover Jackie loved his clothes and liked to be well turned-out. Over time, his wardrobe would expand and his accessories increase, making his closets explode.

I was shocked to learn that occasionally, this clean-cut young man even spent the night sleeping outside when it was warm or in a 24-hour KFC, just to save money. Meanwhile, I was working a regular office job and renting a relatively comfortable two-room apartment in Wangjing with my own kitchen and bathroom.

Jackie said he came from a place close to Xi'an city in northwest China and had a twin sister. He showed me photos of himself in different cities, and said he had been in the army, but had not gone to university. Jackie then demonstrated a soldier's march for me, with his back and legs straight as a rod; he was quite convincing. But actually he had "been to university," as he had worked as a campus security guard at a university, where he met many foreign students and staff. In addition to his extroverted nature, this explained why he felt comfortable approaching foreigners.

"I like Americans' personality because they are friendly," Jackie said simply. I sometimes wondered whether some Chinese really liked Americans, or the stereotypical concept that they represented, a "better" life, freedom, and affluence. Jackie's answer, however, struck me as sincere.

He showed me photos of himself with his foreign friends on his digital camera, which was broken in a corner and fixed with tape. I believed everything he told me, that he had worked as a security guard, did odd jobs such as working at a golf stadium, modeling, or handing out leaflets while wearing a bear and an Ultraman costume. He was now an aspiring actor.

I later heard there were quite a few aspiring actors in Wangjing. Honestly, I didn't buy Jackie's acting story when we first met, but he later showed me photos of himself playing soldiers or doctors on set. When he wasn't acting, he was doing odd jobs and when he wasn't doing odd jobs, he was acting. Jackie was always on the go.

"I have a job interview about every day," Jackie told me.

"Goodness, how exhausting!" I thought to myself.

When I told an American friend about Jackie several months

later, she admitted she had "trouble connecting the dots" as Jackie's life appeared quite unorthodox and confusing, especially to a foreigner unfamiliar with China's migrant workers. They come from China's countryside and smaller cities to the large cities to find luck and fortune, but migrant workers do not enjoy the same privileges as official residents, such as access to social services, medical care, free education, and the right to buy property. The migrant workers in Beijing are known as *beipiao* (北漂 literally means "Beijing drifter").

A fresh wind was rustling through the poplars, and Jackie and I were sitting on newspapers he had spread out on a bench. He took out a notebook, full of names and telephone numbers of contacts, as well as notes. I could hardly decipher them. Like many migrant workers, he relied on his many contacts for work.

Chinese people are usually not so open about their thoughts and feelings and are reluctant to let strangers immediately enter their worlds, but Jackie was different. He pointed to his backpack and said, "This is my life." Always on the move with his odd jobs and acting, he was sometimes gone for months from Beijing before gradually finding his way back, unlike most migrant workers in China who move to a big city and tend to stay for long periods of time. In this sense, Jackie was also more of an exception than the rule in China.

Little did I know that this was the beginning of a fantastic journey for both of us. Like me, Jackie liked philosophizing, using his imagination, picturing the extraordinary; he relished a certain degree of freedom, traveling, a romantic and unfettered life. The fact that we had two different mother tongues and my Chinese wasn't that good was not a deterrent at all and made the encounter all the more charming and occasionally amusing.

I snuck a glance at Jackie's backpack. It was black with a green interior, and inside there were newspapers I would later learn he used to sit on in public places; there was an umbrella, books and his casting card, which he showed me. It featured photos of Jackie playing soldiers, warriors and businessmen. As an American friend of mine in Beijing once observed, "Not being tied to a place, but tied to a mission is the coolest!"

Thus Jackie introduced me to his world. In many ways his world was smaller than mine—he had only taken an airplane once in his life at that point and had never been to other countries. But in other ways it was larger, with his rather rich social and work experience accumulated due to his always being on the move. Meanwhile, while I had traveled extensively in Europe, I had spent quite a while at university, sheltered from society.

I would notice later that Jackie always appeared to be wearing different shoes; as it turned out, although he had few belongings, he did own a number of pairs of shoes. Some Chinese friends had always admired the "free and easy lifestyle" that I enjoyed as a foreigner, mostly unfettered by local social conventions. But Jackie's was even freer than mine, as symbolized by his many pairs of shoes, and it was far from easy. He was free as a bird, yet many tend to forget that freedom always comes at a price. In Jackie's case, it was occasional hardship and the lack of a stable home, but at that point in his life, it didn't appear to bother him in the least.

Jackie told me about his background and how he broke into acting. His father had initially objected to his son pursuing an acting career as he wanted his son to become an official, a wish shared with many Chinese parents, and he had invested his limited resources in sending his son to a good local boarding school not far from home.

But Jackie's talents and interests did not lie in becoming a government official. He said he liked the freedom to move from city to city rather than moving back to his hometown or someplace nearby. "He is sort of like a gypsy or a hobo!" I thought.

Jackie's father eventually resigned himself to his son's life choices. "You are different from other people," his father said; interestingly, my father had always told me the same about myself. I believe in retrospect Jackie felt partly attracted to me precisely because of that, and vice versa.

Jackie was very much focused on his acting career.

"Whatever the mind can conceive and believe, it can achieve," Jackie told me in heavily accented English. I froze, as I had a sense of déjà vu. My father had been a great fan of Napoleon Hill, an American who believed in the power of positive thinking and whom Jackie had just quoted. When I was growing up, my father had always insisted my sister and I as well as select visitors sit on the sofa and listen to his collection of Napoleon Hill's success records.

Jackie was also very much interested in my life, and I told him about it, giving him a *Reader's Digest* version in my limited Chinese. When I mentioned my educational background to him, his eyes popped. "Wow, you have a PhD!" he exclaimed.

Then Jackie pointed to a path leading away from us. "Let's walk part of our way together," he proposed.

When a young coworker later asked me about Jackie's profession, and I replied "actor," he countered, "How do you know he is not putting on an act when he is with you?" That was a legitimate question, but I told him I could tell when the charm was off.

Despite my limited Chinese, more basic communication between Jackie and myself did take place after our first encounter. I had lived in China for three years at that point and had been working on my Chinese, so I was able to handle simple conversations with Jackie. Also, I had previously been to China twice with my former Chinese boyfriend from university in Germany.

Now I was understanding more or less everything that Jackie was saying. "Luckily you can speak some Chinese, else there wouldn't be any communication," Jackie told me.

I felt very distant from my friends in the West and far removed from home, but I was actually enjoying the strange mix of freedom, loneliness and camaraderie that Beijing afforded on that afternoon when I first met Jackie. Granted, the language and cultural barriers occasionally made me feel as if I were an inmate talking to visitors behind bullet-proof glass in a maximum security prison, but I did have breakthroughs when I felt I was actually getting through to the Chinese I interacted with, for example, Jackie. The fact that he spoke slowly, his pronunciation was clear and the vocabulary he used with me was rather simple really enabled us to communicate smoothly. It was a liberation.

The key to making friends everywhere is being patient, open-minded and having the humility to admit your mistakes while maintaining a measure of self-confidence. A sense of humor is vital, too. Jackie gave me a chance to practice these attributes, without which I believe I would have been quickly defeated by Chinese society, which I found occasionally hard to navigate, especially on a deeper level, and I would have returned to my home country with my tail between my legs.

In some ways, my situation and Jackie's mirrored each other's, while in others, they were the opposite. For example, Jackie didn't really know how to read words written in the alphabet system, and had trouble recognizing when letters formed units, a problem he still has. However, he was able to recognize some words, such as "Hello," "China," "Chinese," and "Good morning." Meanwhile, I had the same problems with Chinese characters.

I took a photo of Jackie with my mobile phone on that day, of him flashing a "victory" or "peace" sign, as many Chinese are in the habit of doing when posing for photos. He was dressed in shorts and a black T-shirt bearing the multi-colored Union Jack.

It was in the days before WeChat, so Jackie and I took out our flip phones and exchanged telephone numbers. We shook hands when we parted, and Jackie said, "Goodbye, friend for a lifetime!" I found his hands warm but pretty calloused, indicating he used them for labor. They weren't baby-soft like those of an office worker. I caught a whiff of cheap soap from his hand-washed shirt that briefly mingled with the big city smells of car fumes and sewers.

I was puzzled and intrigued by my new acquaintance. "This thing with Jackie—I don't know what it is!" I wrote in my diary around that time. But no matter what it was, I believed "every person is a potential gift."

At that point, after three years in China, I had had only very limited interactions with what one could call blue-collar workers, as I mostly worked and interacted with college graduates and white-collar members of society. Interactions with blue-collar workers occurred usually when running errands or when engaging in small talk, for example, with janitors or cleaning ladies.

I did, however, make a successful effort to reach out to the security guards in my first Beijing neighborhood of Liufang (柳芳), before moving to Wangjing and eventually meeting Jackie. Let me recount one episode here with a security guard, Jackie's occupation before he became an aspiring actor.

I was appalled at the living conditions of our security guards in Liufang. On my trips to the management office to have things fixed, I noticed they slept in bunk beds in dank, windowless rooms in the basement and their bathroom was primitive. Little did I know Jackie was living in similarly modest facilities in Beijing's Bayi Film Lot around the same time I was living in Liufang, when he was trying to break into the acting industry. But at that time, of course, we hadn't met and moved to Wangjing.

I was sleeping in a queen-sized bed with a warm western exposure and taking hot showers in my roomy shower stall, while fifteen floors beneath me, life looked a lot less cheerful.

On one occasion, I had tried to offer one security guard at my complex some fine European chocolates, but he immediately hid in the guardhouse like a hermit crab in its shell.

"Tamara, many Chinese just don't have experience with foreigners and therefore don't know how to interact with them," a Chinese friend explained.

I was not discouraged. On the evening of the Chinese Mid-Autumn Festival, it is customary to look at the full moon, so I took a walk that evening and photographed the moon peeping out through the branches of the willow trees; after all, I was living in Liufang, the "fragrant willow" neighborhood of Beijing. Then I walked back to my apartment building. Before entering my compound, I stopped at the shabby office desk in front of the guardhouse, and the guard on duty was the same one I had previously frightened with the chocolates. This time his reaction was different, as he clearly recognized me, the foreign woman who had offered him chocolates. An American coworker was right when he had said, "Chinese don't forget a *laowai*" (colloquial Chinese for "foreigner").

"The poor man," I thought. "It must be sad and lonely working as a security guard on a night like this, away from home and family. After all, it's the Mid-Autumn Festival, the Chinese Thanksgiving."

I decided not to traumatize him with my Chinese but I reached into one of my coat pockets, and silently held out my hands, holding a gift.

 The guard's face lit up like a paper lantern as he, with both hands, accepted the two moon cakes I was offering him. (In China, it is more polite to give and receive gifts with two hands than with one, and that especially applies to exchanging business cards, just as it is sometimes better to give multiples of small gifts instead of just one, with even numbers being preferred.)

 I fled, not wanting to cause any further embarrassment. As I was hurrying away, I heard the English words "Thank you" spoken softly with a Chinese lilt.

 China was opening its arms.

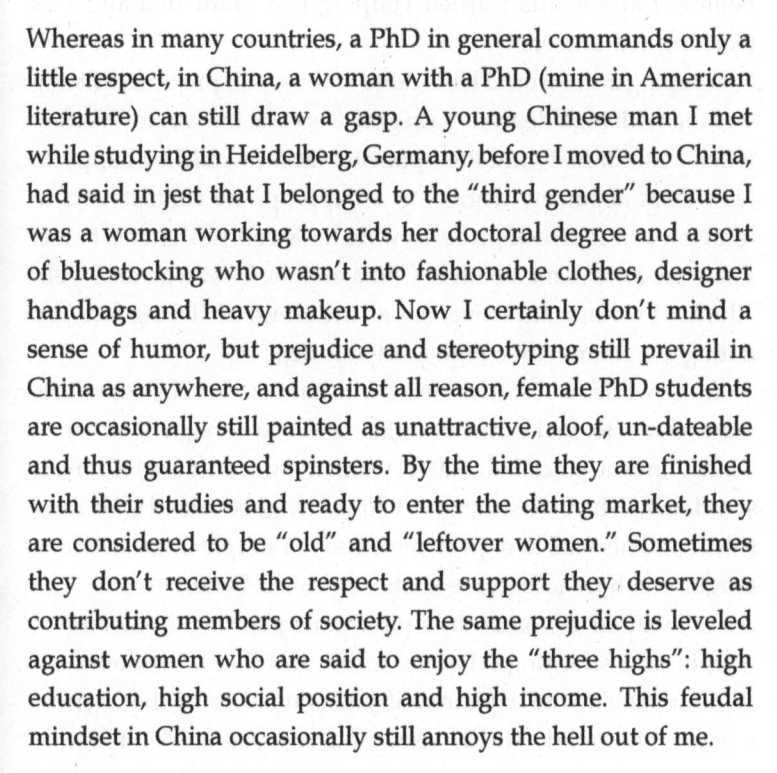

Whereas in many countries, a PhD in general commands only a little respect, in China, a woman with a PhD (mine in American literature) can still draw a gasp. A young Chinese man I met while studying in Heidelberg, Germany, before I moved to China, had said in jest that I belonged to the "third gender" because I was a woman working towards her doctoral degree and a sort of bluestocking who wasn't into fashionable clothes, designer handbags and heavy makeup. Now I certainly don't mind a sense of humor, but prejudice and stereotyping still prevail in China as anywhere, and against all reason, female PhD students are occasionally still painted as unattractive, aloof, un-dateable and thus guaranteed spinsters. By the time they are finished with their studies and ready to enter the dating market, they are considered to be "old" and "leftover women." Sometimes they don't receive the respect and support they deserve as contributing members of society. The same prejudice is leveled against women who are said to enjoy the "three highs": high education, high social position and high income. This feudal mindset in China occasionally still annoys the hell out of me.

HUTONG HEARTTHROBS

No doubt this prejudice and stereotyping originated from members of society who are intimidated by well-educated, empowered women. But my Chinese friend Haiping (海平), a woman of humble origins from Shandong province, had one of the "three highs" and was on her way to obtaining at least a "second high." She was a strong-spirited, focused woman who had worked hard to get where she was, and she wasn't fazed by relatives who requested her to "show us your boyfriend." She was amused she had once been mistaken for a masseuse because of her voluptuous figure. She would go on to earn her PhD in German art and its impact on Chinese painting at the Central Academy of Fine Arts (CAFA), a prestigious arts academy in Beijing. I afterwards learned Haiping had graduated and was teaching at a university.

Haiping and I would have none of the social prejudices facing women with high degrees; I am glad to say Jackie wouldn't either when I met him. Quite the opposite, Jackie would be happy to tell others about my degree, in an appropriate context, and to him, it was a source of pride, as were his accomplishments to me. There are always men both in China and the West who find well-educated women attractive; not all are afraid of "losing face" by dating a woman with a high academic degree.

Meanwhile, well-intentioned, but not very successful efforts were made to make me, a rather average foreign woman in China, into a so-called better woman by traditional Chinese standards. When I first came to China, my good friend Guo Yang (果阳) and his wife had given me a book in simple Chinese which taught one how to become such a so-called better woman. The cover featured a woman in a pink tunic painting a bluebird of happiness, a snoozing cat in the corner and cherry blossoms.

Guo Yang's wife explained if you wanted to be the "perfect woman" by traditional Chinese standards, you needed to know how to cook and have good social and conversational skills.

Next to holding down a career and being a good wife and mother, she herself met both requirements. I was becoming better at my social skills since leaving the ivory tower of university and not just hiding behind my desk, but I hated small-talk and cooking. Luckily, Jackie, a chatterbox, is happy to oblige by doing the cooking when he is home in the hutong house we later rented and by helping me improve my Chinese social skills. To this day, I remain a "work in progress" in becoming a "better Chinese woman." Still, you can't square a circle. I obviously wasn't a Chinese woman in the first place and what's more, in some ways I wasn't a traditional woman.

To Jackie, my PhD was initially a marvel, like my big nose, "cherry lips," as he described them, and blue eyes, just as his acting vocation, lifestyle and adventures fascinated me, but after we got to know each other, these simply became parts of each other's identity we came to accept. And my being almost four years older than Jackie is not much of a big deal in today's China, where men are expected to be traditionally older than their spouses. We met when I was 34 and he was 31.

I saw Jackie several times after our first encounter because he lived in the same neighborhood. Many people both in China and the West meet their significant others at parties, social events, at work, or nowadays, online, either by themselves or through matchmaking services. Facebook founder Mark Zuckerberg met his future wife Priscilla Chan, a Chinese American, while standing in line for the restroom at a party at Harvard University. A young foreign man in China met his Chinese girlfriend, a doctor, while getting a health check. Not super romantic, but it worked for them. Jackie and I saw each other's reflections in a subway car window and sparks flew.

The traditional approach, in China especially, is having

friends or family members play the role of matchmaker and that's how Jackie's parents met. But the subway as Cupid? Pretty strange. The typical reactions I get are "How romantic!" and "It's like in the movies."

Life does work in mysterious ways. What I didn't realize then was that riding just one stop on Line 15 of the Beijing subway for five minutes on May 9, 2012, was going to change my life forever. As Jackie said later, "一站，一辈子" (*Yi zhan, yi beizi*), meaning one stop determining the rest of your life. If I hadn't been working the morning shift that day and Jackie hadn't been let off early after a modeling stint at a university (the art students were painting his head as he had classic features), our paths would never have crossed. If he or I had been delayed five minutes, or maybe just one minute, and not stepped into the same subway car. . .

I doubt my life would have been as exciting and rewarding if I hadn't met Jackie; I might have returned to my native US, held an office job, and led a very conventional, boring, white-collar life, without ever returning to China.

Once, Jackie and I were eating fries at a KFC. While KFC has been in the US for decades, the first KFC in China opened its doors only in the late 1980s, even before McDonald's and the first Walmart arrived in the 1990s. An American friend who visited Beijing as a child shortly after the opening-up process began in the 1980s told his teacher in the US that Beijing was wonderful, except that he missed McDonald's. When my friend visited Beijing again in 2019 as a grown man, he was amazed at the transformation.

My Beijing neighborhood at that time, Wangjing, which was ultra-modern and home to many tech companies, had both a KFC and a Walmart, which made me feel especially at home because of the convenience of getting Western-style foods and goods if I had the urge. To Jackie, they were still somewhat of a novelty.

Jackie squeezed a pack of ketchup over his KFC fries. "How do you eat French fries in the US?" he asked.

"Just like in China," I laughed and told him about KFC's founder Colonel Sanders and how he had been a customer at my maternal grandparents' liquor store. He really did wear a white suit and bought chewing gum.

"Wow, really?" Jackie was surprised at this.

"Why do foreigners have such big noses?" Jackie then asked. (Later, he would even compare my nose to an elephant's trunk or the "nose" of a plane.)

"Well, why do Chinese have such small noses?" I countered, grinning. We laughed.

"Is life in the US hard?" Jackie asked.

"That depends," I said. Life can land a punch on anyone, anywhere whether in the US or China; there are impoverished people in both countries. Jackie continued to munch thoughtfully on the fries. Lack of information often leads to misconceptions, so a lot of what Chinese know about life in the West comes from the media, such as TV shows and movies. The same, of course, applies to Westerners' knowledge of China, though it's more extensive and analytical.

I saw Jackie again when he came back from an acting stint out of town. He was wearing a sunhat and his arms glowed.

"Jackie, what happened to your arms?" I asked, alarmed. A nasty sunburn was flowering on his upper arms, and the skin had started to peel. I rushed to the nearest pharmacy to get him some salve and sunscreen. I washed his sunburns using fresh wipes in place of disinfectant, then dabbed the salve on the wounded skin. Jackie barely flinched.

All the while, he was watching me with warm, friendly eyes. He struck me as being full of childlike innocence and very trusting, at least towards me.

"You should take better care of yourself!" I admonished him, and gave him the salve and the sunscreen for future use.

Jackie's attitude regarding the sunburn was that it didn't matter too much and could actually help him land the role of a soldier he wanted to audition for, as it would make him appear steeled and toughened.

Already, it was obvious that Jackie was an optimistic and happy-go-lucky person and someone who didn't complain, whereas I am an occasional worrywart and complainer and someone who thinks things over twice or thrice before making a move. Life to Jackie was something to be embraced and enjoyed; to me, it was occasionally serious business, to be faced head-on as a never-ending series of challenges and problems.

Not too long afterward, I saw Jackie again. He was wearing a suit and tie and had just come back from an audition. I suppressed a laugh when I saw him swaggering a bit. When we found a bench, Jackie took out a newspaper from his backpack so we could sit on it, as I had noticed was his habit.

He took off his jacket, rolled up his shirt sleeves and showed me his arms. They were nicely healed. Now, they looked fine and smooth as baby's skin. Jackie's given name, "Peng" (鹏), means a "large, fabulous bird, roc" and that he is. There's a popular Chinese proverb that literally means "the roc journeys ten thousand *li* (miles)" (鹏程万里), which means to enjoy brilliant prospects.

Jackie noticed my shoes were dusty, and he stooped down and used a fresh wipe to clean them. I told him to please stand up, as I found it a bit embarrassing. My father always used to polish my shoes before I went to school or for special occasions, and today, here was Jackie carrying on the tradition. There was no way I could dissuade him. Jackie was very clean and neat, except for occasionally spitting on the street, a habit of many Chinese. Spitting or blowing one's nose on the street has ancient roots in traditional medicine; it is to rid the body of toxins. But today it is discouraged for health reasons and because it comes across as bad manners and conveys a bad image. Most young city people in China don't spit or snort.

No banquet lasts forever, and the same could be said about my first stint in China. A coworker had taught me the expression "fallen leaves return to their roots" (落叶归根), meaning one usually eventually returns to one's place of origin.

Shortly before meeting Jackie, I had accepted a job back in San Francisco and signed a work contract, plus my father wasn't in good health, and I wanted to be closer to him. I had experienced enough adventures during my three years in China to fill a book, and was loathe to leave behind my colorful life in Beijing. But duty called. I was somewhat heartbroken.

As my plane was lifting off for San Francisco, I pictured Jackie down below in our Wangjing neighborhood, hand-washing his clothes in a bathroom sink in the apartment he shared with five other men. Truthfully, I had absolutely no idea what the future would bring, and had no expectations. I was needed back home and had a new job as well. I didn't have the luxury or time of really indulging in any sentimentality. That would come later.

I never forgot Jackie after I left China in 2012, although at that time I had only known him briefly. After I got to the US, I sometimes wondered how he was doing and hoped he was taking good care of himself half a world away. I assumed we would never see each other again, and that our relationship, tenuous as it was, would fade. My friend and pen pal Beixi (贝茜) from Singapore, whom I had met in Beijing when she was a medical student there, thought the same about Jackie. Roughly ten years my junior, Beixi was a gifted student, precocious and wise beyond her years.

"It's a short episode in the general scheme of things," she emailed me, which struck me as a rational, cool-headed approach. But she added, "People never really leave us if we want them to stay." I found that thought comforting.

Jackie and I stayed in touch. He would write emails from internet cafés from time to time, telling me about his latest acting stints. Again, this was in the days before WeChat and all the similar social media apps, which today make life so much more convenient with video chats and phone calls possible anywhere, often free. Jackie did not own a computer, and wasn't really computer literate, so usually the only way to access his emails was in internet cafés. Not owning a computer might be inconceivable to people like me who enjoy a white-collar life and rely on computers for work, communication with friends, online banking and everything else. But Jackie made do.

Little did I know he was also carrying a photo of both of us in his wallet, next to a photo of himself with the Chinese superstar Jackie Chan. Carrying photos of loved ones or special people in one's wallet is definitely an American habit, and several years later I asked Jackie about it.

"I must have gotten the idea from a Hollywood movie," he admitted. "Chinese are reserved; they usually only carry cash in their wallets." Not their hearts, that's what he meant.

TAMMY TREICHEL

I closed my eyes as I reclined in my plane seat and the events of the last month passed like film footage in front of my mind's eye. The second-to-last time I met with Jackie it had been raining heavily, but now the sun had come out. He was sweaty in a white shirt and black suit, and had just come from an acting stint. He also appeared taller than I remembered him to be, and only later would I learn that he would occasionally wear shoe inserts to enhance his height for acting work.

As he approached, he handed me a plastic bag as a farewell gift. I peeked inside and very carefully took out its contents, making sure not to prick my fingers. "Hah, a cactus!" I exclaimed. I was surprised and amused at first, then touched.

I was reminded of the little girl Gertie in the movie *E.T. the Extra-Terrestrial*, who gifts the alien, E.T. with a plant before he departs for his home planet via spaceship. Only the difference was that here, I couldn't take the plant with me to the US because of customs and agriculture regulations. I told Jackie as much.

"I know," Jackie replied, but he explained he still had bought it because of its little flowers which were a substitute for a bouquet, and that he had been in a supermarket and pressed for time.

When I waxed sentimental and suggested I plant the cactus in the park where we had first met, as a sort of memento, Jackie shook his head, because he felt it would be a waste, so finally we agreed he would give it to one of his neighbors. He then pulled out a little bag with a pearl-studded headband in it because he noticed I was in the habit of wearing headbands in my short hair. Now this was something more useful that I could easily take back with me as a souvenir!

Despite Jackie's obvious hardships, I would come to the conclusion that he was a *kaixinguo* (开心果), which literally means a "pistachio nut," a Chinese term for someone who is amusing and gives happiness to others.

HUTONG HEARTTHROBS

The last time I saw Jackie before leaving for the US, we were taking the escalator down to Line 15 of the Beijing subway. Jackie pointed to the spot where he had first set eyes on me, at the foot of the escalator, not in the subway car itself. He said he had seen my short hair first, which he described as a "mushroom head" or a lady's hairstyle from a classic movie. "Your haircut and temperament attracted me," he admitted many years later. "I was curious to see what your face looked like."

"I feel like I have known you a long time. You have given me the greatest happiness in Beijing," he said, and I could see his eyes glazing over with unshed tears.

One Chinese acquaintance told me that it was best not to express too much joy or sorrow before others, but I am not sure whether that explained the many poker faces I had seen during my time in China. Maybe the poker faces were due to the fact that many Chinese are more reserved in public because they tend to be more suspicious, and not showing emotions was a way of protecting themselves. Now, Jackie was clearly an exception with his expressive face. And as an actor, you need to be able to show emotions, and let your face and eyes do a lot of the talking.

"Take care of yourself in the US, and come back to China, the sooner, the better," he said. Upon parting, he and I turned around and waved to each other. Not only once, but twice. Then three times.

Not too long later, my mobile phone glowed. It was Jackie. "I'll wait for your return to China."

I just replied with one Chinese character that denotes "return."

2

"Different from other people"

I suppose wanderlust runs in my family. My family has been moving or has been moved around quite a bit.

My mother, Joan, grew up in Louisville, Kentucky, during the 1940s and 1950s. Louisville was a sleepy, rather boring southern city in those years. But my mother set her sights on living in Paris, France, where she studied during her second year in college.

My father, Horst, meanwhile, was growing up in Pomerania, Germany (now part of Poland), in much more dramatic circumstances. As Germany started to lose World War II and the

Russians moved in, my father and his mother, brother, and sister managed to catch the last train to western Germany, with the Russians shooting after the train, hitting and derailing one of the train cars. My father and his family were placed with a farming family in a town near Bremen. This was quite a come-down from their upper-class background.

In the late 1950s, my father's brother, Uncle Siegfried, went to the US for a medical internship and residency. After suffering in war-ravaged Germany, he was so gung-ho about the US that he suggested my father move there as well. My father agreed, had to serve in the US military for six months and was posted in Fort Knox, Kentucky. He met my mother at a dance in Louisville. After introductions, my father, a handsome blond, blue-eyed German, clicked his heels together and made a little bow toward my mother. German men did such things in those years. Both would discover they shared a passion for ballroom dancing.

Yes, my mother was smitten! But it was also the start of a romance that ebbed and flowed for a decade as my father became a shipbroker in Baltimore and my mother a journalist in New York City. She had enjoyed a colorful variety of dates that eventually frustrated her father. Finally, after about ten years of an on-again, off-again romance, my parents married in Washington, D.C., in 1972, after my mother cheekily encouraged my father to propose in the back of a London taxi cab. I would say they had a happy marriage and complemented each other in unexpected ways while sticking to shared goals.

My mother was a free spirit who studied belly dancing for fun, wore pigtails into adulthood and quit work to travel Europe, where she fell in love with an engineering student in what was formerly East Germany. This "forbidden love" behind the Iron Curtain was doomed from the very beginning, and sadly, the student was expelled from university as a result, but it set the stage for my mother's then falling for my father. Later, she tried to charm snakes and painted the brick fireplace a daredevil color—turquoise. She always said, "Children, do what's right for you."

By contrast, my father was more old-school and conservative. As a shipbroker, he owned his own company for a while. He was a self-made man, an immigrant who lived the American Dream and a die-hard fan of Fox News, an ultra-conservative TV channel in the US. He loved American politics but did not want to get involved and give up his German citizenship, keeping it as a potential exit option for his family. My father had a somewhat neo-Cold War mentality, yet he approved of my going to China to work back in 2009 as an editor. And when I was dating my first boyfriend, a young Chinese fellow student, he accepted it. When one of my German cousins called up my father and asked whether he approved of my dating a Chinese man, my father staunchly replied, "Tammy may date whomever she pleases."

Politically, my mother was more liberal, and as a journalist she wanted to ensure my father got "balanced" news, so she made him watch a more liberal news channel for at least thirty minutes every day. But while she was preparing meals in the kitchen during commercials, my father would snatch the remote control and secretly switch back to Fox News until my mother returned to the living room, before which he quickly switched back to a liberal news channel. That was pretty much the only power struggle between them that I was aware of.

My parents made Washington, D.C., their home, and I was born there. I grew up bilingually. So I spent my childhood and youth switching gears between two different languages, cultures, countries (the US and Germany) and continents. That predestined me to be a globetrotter and sparked my curiosity in different cultures as well as my willingness to assimilate.

HUTONG HEARTTHROBS

Although it is a gift from my parents to have been raised bilingually, this bicultural heritage also highlighted cultural differences between Germans and Americans that can be a bit difficult to navigate. I sometimes felt as if I were sitting between two chairs, and not properly on one. I was unseated several times! But in the end, I came to accept and appreciate the differences more than I was annoyed by them, and it significantly softened the culture shock I experienced in China.

When traveling and studying in Germany, I was accepted into the fold with my nearly flawless German. Meanwhile, back in the US, people would ask me, "Where are you from?" When I replied, "Washington, D.C.," they would look at me askance and ask, "Where are you *really* from?" I suspect it might be because I look more European.

My first boss when I got to Beijing, a Chinese man, seemed disappointed when he first saw me at the airport. "You don't look American," he said in an uncharacteristically frank manner. "But you look better than on your passport photo."

On the whole, however, I feel better in China than I did in the US or Germany in terms of identity. Whereas in the West I always felt I was straddling two sides, in China, my role is clearly defined: I play "the foreigner" and am at complete liberty to create and recreate my role, both literally and metaphorically.

My parents even visited me in China in 2011. It was my father's first and last trip to Asia before he died in 2015. I'm glad I was there when he passed. Confucius said, "While your parents are alive, don't venture too far."

My father's death from cancer reinforced my sense of *carpe diem*—the importance of leading a meaningful, fulfilling life every day. My father had always been supportive of my creative projects, no matter how hare-brained or exotic — a costly study tour to St. Petersburg, Russia, to learn more about the Russian Imperial Family, the Romanovs; or my PhD thesis on Herman Melville's *Moby Dick*, which my father, not surprisingly, found a hard read, and, of course, my first stint working in China.

My father would shake his head occasionally and say, "Tammy, Tammy, you are different from other people."

His initial suspicion gradually turned into respect after he had interacted with Chinese people.

As my father lay dying, we talked a bit about China, also known as the "Middle Kingdom" (in Chinese, China literally means "Country in the Middle").

"Move me to the middle of the bed," he said.

"*Reich der Mitte* (German for 'Middle Kingdom')," he added, gently.

"I miss China," I admitted.

"I know," he replied.

After my father's death, I moved back to China in the spring of 2015, and worked as an editor at the same organization where I had worked earlier. It was a homecoming, and a distraction from the sorrow over my father's departure.

However, before I moved back to China for my second work stint, I experienced a few detours. In 2012, I moved to San Francisco, California to work at a book publisher before moving to Houston, Texas. In San Francisco, I had a boring 9-5 *Office Space*-type of job. Although I had my own office instead of a cubicle, I found myself wanting to kick the crap out of a printer and hoard a red stapler.

Later, I got a job as a leasing agent at a distress property called Arcadia at Westheimer in Houston. I initially enjoyed the adrenaline rush and "entertainment" offered by Arcadia before understanding the full implications of my job.

HUTONG HEARTTHROBS

I befriended another leasing agent called Sherry, a kind-hearted African-American woman who abhorred the little lies that come with a sales job. We comforted each other and wiped each other's tears when things were going badly. Now this wasn't the first time I was working in an environment where I as a white person was in the minority, the first time was in Beijing from 2009-2012. At Arcadia, I worked with African-Americans and Latinos; after all, Houston is a diverse American city. The residents called me "The Lady in the Buick" because I roared in to work over the potholes in a banged-up blue, third-hand Buick that no one would want to steal or break into.

Arcadia at Westheimer certainly didn't live up to its name from Greek mythology as it wasn't bucolic in the least; it was an apartment complex bastion with many disgruntled blue-collar residents who put up with crime, drugs and maintenance problems on a daily basis. One resident was allowed to get out of her lease early because there were snakes in her toilet, while another called me up to complain about a bat being stuck in her chimney. A postal worker always dumped all the residents' packages in our leasing office and then sped away in his truck because he was terrified of being solicited by drug dealers.

Most tragically, however, a woman I had moved into the complex was shot dead on the property grounds by her estranged ex-husband. Like many local Texans, my coworker Sherry owned a gun and could shoot. "Tamara, do you know how to shoot? Where's your gun?" she asked me one day as some outraged residents were storming our office due to a maintenance problem. As Sherry and I were cowering behind our desks, I didn't know how to respond as I did not feel comfortable owning a "killing machine," even though we were living in trigger-happy Texas. Well, shooting or being shot wouldn't be a concern once I moved back to China; plenty of other challenges would be waiting for me there.

As trying as my time at Arcadia was, it taught me a lot of things I did not learn at university. For one, next to my experience in China, it helped me acquire more street smarts after having grown up in a relatively drama-free, upper-middle class, mostly white surrounding. A neighbor of my parents called Jill told my mother, "Now Tammy knows how the other half (of America) lives." As Arcadia's exceptionally smart property manager, Joy, who had just about seen it all, taught me, "Don't assume anything."

I can't pinpoint the moment when I became fascinated with China. There wasn't a single defining moment. There were bits and pieces of China everywhere as if I were sweeping them up from a shattered mirror.

There was a photo of me looking like Little Lord Fauntleroy as a small child, as I had short hair and usually wore pants, appearing rather ready for mischief next to a Happy Buddha at a Chinese restaurant. Then there were the pre-teen years when I frequented a store owned by a Chinese couple. I loved their Chinese knickknacks, but was somewhat turned off by their sour attitude and a handwritten sign with the words, "We break, we cry. You break, you buy!" But I remember having bought a tacky dragon figurine there, sandalwood soap and cloth shoes that were surprisingly big enough for my large feet and very comfortable; I wore them until they were threadbare.

In high school, I became obsessed with a silent movie from 1919 called *Broken Blossoms*. I played the film over and over on our VCR. It was cathartic, it was super depressing, it was the perfect outlet for my teenage angst. It starred my favorite actress, Lillian Gish, with her shower of ash-blond curls and blue-gray eyes that she really knew how to widen in shock. In *Broken Blossoms*, Gish plays a girl called Lucy who is repeatedly beaten by her alcoholic father, a professional boxer in London's slum-like, blue-collar Limehouse District. However, Lucy is loved by a Chinese man, a shopkeeper who feels lonely and alienated in his new country (due to prevailing norms at the time, the Chinese protagonist was played by a white actor, Richard Barthelmess), who treats her with gentleness and kindness. Of course, it was 1919, so this love story remained "pure" and unconsummated. You won't see more than a kiss on the forehead or the gifting of a doll here. For its time, surely, *Broken Blossoms* was not only a cinematic masterpiece where mood and lighting were concerned, but also a risqué and progressive film due to its depiction of an interracial relationship.

There was also a large, intricate Chinese autumn landscape print I had hung in my bedroom when I was in high school. I remember my mother's relief when I took it down as she thought it was schlock.

What really drew me to China the first time were Chinese friends who left favorable impressions of the country, as well as my first Chinese boyfriend whom I met while studying in Heidelberg, Germany. Thanks to him, I visited China twice before actually moving here to work. He urged me to "open your heart." He had pried open a door for me and I stepped through. And I think I thus became more open and receptive to other people, cultures and places.

A Chinese friend from university predicted, "You will meet many interesting people in China." Among them, of course, was a colorful, aspiring actor called Jackie.

3

A JACK OF MANY TRADES

So who is this Chinese man who captured my heart? What was his life like, half a world away, prior to his life with me?

Having worked a dizzying array of jobs around China, Jackie is indeed a jack of many trades. In Beijing, I once met the British writer Andrew Hicks, who has put together the book *Jack Jones: A True Friend to China*. Jack Jones was a veritable British "Jack of all trades" who had stints working on a fishing trawler, in a sugar beet factory, as a potato digger and a speedway rider before becoming a volunteer in China, providing medical relief in the 1940s. Hicks wrote to me, "It was a very great pleasure meeting you and always inspiring to meet someone who is living so exciting and different a life to the usual conventional treadmill of life in the West." And that was even truer of my Jackie. He more or less remembers each of his stints, with Shanghai a vivid example.

"My Shanghai work was to call customers nonstop to enroll in corporate courses. We would call in a crazy manner after being inspired every day in the morning meetings," Jackie recalled. It sounded like something out of *The Wolf of Wall Street*, the Leonardo DiCaprio movie. Jackie couldn't stand the cold, damp Shanghai winter; it made him sick and he left.

When Jackie was growing up in Yang County (洋县) near Xi'an, in Shaanxi province, he was introverted and hid from visitors to his home—a far cry from his extroverted personality today. He wasn't interested in school, and in junior middle school, he was focused only on his pretty English teacher. He then studied at Hanzhong Sports College, worked as a server at a hotpot restaurant and a tea house in Hanzhong city, not far from his home, and as an assistant at a wedding photography company. Then he studied martial arts. In Xi'an he worked for two years as a security guard at a supermarket.

He joined the military, the Chinese Special Armed Police in Sichuan province and enjoyed it, especially drills with his comrades-in-arms, jogging with them at Mount Cuiping in Yibin.

On the day he was discharged from the military in November 2005, his instructor lectured, "You are all kids with a naughty streak who didn't go to university, who didn't study well; your economic conditions might not have been good... I hope now you will enroll in university or find other opportunities to study. I hope you won't become security guards!" Of course, this was a gross oversimplification of army recruits. Jackie, however, followed his instructor's words to the letter. He would go to university and "study" — ironically, while working as a security guard.

After being discharged from the military and spending two months with his parents during the Spring Festival (Chinese New Year) in 2006, Jackie's father suddenly told Jackie, "Next month, I'm asking you to pay rent!" To Jackie, this was unexpected, but to me, his father sounded like an American parent.

Several days later found Jackie at the train station. It was a toss-up between going to Beijing or Guangzhou in Guangdong province. He chose Guangzhou simply because he couldn't afford a train ticket to Beijing. The slow train to Guangzhou took 24 hours. He worked for a week at a clothing warehouse, sleeping among jeans, then worked at a shoe factory assembly line in Shenzhen. After he quit, he went to an internet café and learned Guangdong University of Foreign Studies (广东外语外贸大学, "Guangwai" for short) needed a security guard. He landed the job.

As a security guard, Jackie shared a room with three others, slept in a bunk bed and ate in the canteen, like the university students. During the day, he was expected to stand, but at night he could sit down. He got around on a second-hand bicycle, and went through three bicycles during his four years at Guangwai.

As a security guard, Jackie met all kinds of people — students and teachers, both Chinese and foreign — and helped with the one-month compulsory military training of university freshmen because of his military background, which was a source of pride.

His job, however, was not only ensuring campus security but occasionally calling a taxi; this was in the days before Uber and Didi. This would prove a problem on one occasion when the English word "*taxi*" was used.

"While I was at my post, standing next to the south gate of

the university, a young man addressed me with one word: 'taxi.' I didn't know what 'taxi' was! So I just continued to stare at him. You can imagine, I was rooted to the spot. Why? Because I didn't know what he was saying. What was a taxi? The young man repeated 'taxi' five times, when saying the word for the fifth time, he lost his temper. I didn't understand at that time why he was so angry; his face had turned red. I looked at him from top to bottom. He was Japanese."

"At that moment two of his classmates—two Chinese women—came out of the gate and became aware of our communication problem. One of the young women turned to me and said in Chinese, 'He needs a taxi.' Oh, he was saying he needed a taxi! I then got out my walkie-talkie and said, 'Calling west gate, calling west gate. We need a taxi at the south gate! Thank you!' Several minutes later, the Japanese student got into his cab and left."

Jackie finally realized the value of English. "English can solve a lot of life and work problems," he said. "After that episode, I gradually realized its importance. I found my own methods of studying English. The first was watching movies. I started watching American and British movies, because I wanted to listen to authentic English, not Chinglish or English spoken by Chinese. I wanted to learn what English really was like. There were a lot of internet cafés, so I went online and searched for American or British films such as those from the BBC, English-language tapes, *Forrest Gump* and *Lord of the Rings*. Because I was a big fan of Jackie Chan films, I watched his movies in English."

His efforts paid off. "After a while, English sounded so elegant and pleasant that I slowly took a liking to it. Only when I was working as a security guard did I get a feel for what English really was, developed a strong interest and sensed its beauty. So I listened attentively to English-language movies, the pronunciation of American actors and how they delivered their lines. I slowly watched, and slowly listened, again and again. When I recall that period of my life, I was just like a university student. Those were very happy times!"

Jackie frequently wrote down every English sentence and read it out loud several times. He even shouted sentences out loud, and when he was at work, he tested his English on foreign students. They were very nice and listened attentively. Occasionally, they would also flatter Jackie by saying, "Your English is very good!" Wow, that was the first time foreigners had praised Jackie, and he was ecstatic. At Guangwai, Jackie was given the nickname "Crazy Security Guard" because of his single-minded devotion to learning English.

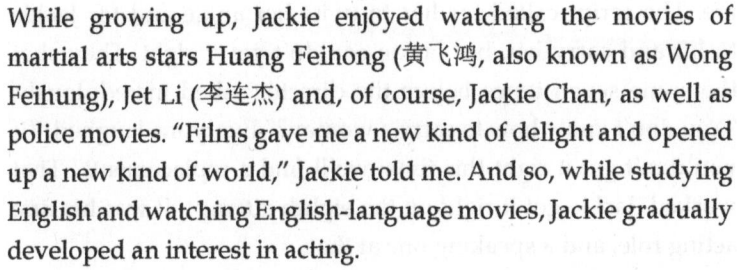

―――∽∽∽―――

While growing up, Jackie enjoyed watching the movies of martial arts stars Huang Feihong (黄飞鸿, also known as Wong Feihung), Jet Li (李连杰) and, of course, Jackie Chan, as well as police movies. "Films gave me a new kind of delight and opened up a new kind of world," Jackie told me. And so, while studying English and watching English-language movies, Jackie gradually developed an interest in acting.

After he had worked at Guangdong University of Foreign Studies for four and a half years, he decided to change jobs and moved to Beijing to break into the acting industry. Prior to that, he had his first encounter with the movie industry in Guangzhou.

On Jackie's birthday in 2009, he decided to do something special: take the day off and visit the Pearl River Film Studio, where he stumbled into an audition and was given an opportunity to audition himself. Although he didn't land a role, he did find a friend and future mentor called Mr. Hu, who told him he needed a resume. The ones he saw featured a lot of photos.

"Little Liu," said Mr. Hu, using his nickname for Jackie ("Liu" or 刘 is Jackie's surname). "If you like to act in movies, you should go to Beijing!" Later, Mr. Hu called Jackie, asking, "Can you play badminton? Do you have a pair of shorts? Do you have sports shoes? And do you have time tomorrow?" After Jackie had answered "yes" to everything, he was sent his lines via QQ, an instant messaging app.

When Jackie arrived on set the next day, he realized he had forgotten his sports shoes. Director Li Hong (李虹) immediately gave his shoes to Jackie—fortunately, they fit—and shooting started.

There were three scenes, one and three went well but the second scene proved problematic. Jackie was to coach the leading lady in playing badminton. Her name was Kong Yingzhi (孔盈智), whose English name in real life is "Tammy," which tickled me. The script called for her to twist her ankle and for Jackie to lift and carry her, but Jackie couldn't get it right. They shot the scene seven times before the director asked incredulously, "You don't know how to carry a woman?" Everyone laughed. "If you don't get it right this time, we'll find a replacement!" That worked. Jackie got it right on the eighth attempt. It was his first acting role, and a speaking one at that.

When he next visited Mr. Hu, he asked Jackie, "What, haven't you left for Beijing?" After pondering this and watching a 2006 TV series called *Soldiers' Sortie* (士兵突击) featuring comedic star Wang Baoqiang (王宝强), who had also found his acting luck in Beijing, Jackie mustered up his courage. He departed for China's capital to pursue his acting dream.

"I remember shouting, 'Beijing, I am coming!'" he told me. "I was so excited."

In October 2010, Jackie took a train from Guangzhou to Beijing, carrying with him three book bags and two heavy suitcases. While queuing, he asked a young man to help him with his luggage and the young man agreed. On the train, Jackie bought him a bottle of water to say thank you. Twenty-four hours later, they arrived at Beijing West Railway Station. The young man helped again, and they exited the station together.

They decided to go job hunting together. Jackie stored his luggage at the station and only took his most important belongings and a small waist bag.

They went to the Bayi Film Studio in Fengtai District. They knocked on the door and said they had come to audition. Applicants went in one by one. Jackie entered first and asked the young man to look after his small waist bag.

After ten minutes, Jackie had wrapped up his audition and returned to the lobby, but the young man and the bag were gone.

Jackie ran his hand over every pocket of his clothes and discovered he had only three yuan (less than USD 0.50) left. Using one yuan, he called his parents using a public phone, saying he had lost his stuff, his ID, his military discharge papers, mobile phone, watch, and several hundred yuan. He was told to transfer 300 yuan (a little under USD 50) to a certain bank account. Why? Because when he was auditioning, he was told, "You look good, you're hired, but we need you to pay a 300 yuan fee up front." Jackie had no choice but to ask his parents for money. "I wasn't afraid of being penniless, but if I had no ID card, I couldn't go anywhere in Beijing," Jackie told me.

He used the second yuan to take the bus to Beijing West Railway Station to pick up his luggage. Without his ID, Jackie had to name the contents of his luggage to prove ownership. He used the third yuan to return to where he had just auditioned. He said he had lost his things — he couldn't say they were stolen. They didn't believe him. Finally, he said he had deposited 300 yuan into their bank account, and they confirmed it. Then they gave him a piece of paper with the name of a firm, the address and telephone number, as well as 20 yuan (about USD 3) as a transportation fee. Jackie later admitted to me he knew he was being cheated by having to pay to land a job, but he was desperate and had no other place to stay in Beijing.

Jackie boarded the bus to the address written on the slip of paper. As the bus was rolling along, he discovered he had left the city center and saw low buildings with red brick walls. He assumed they had arrived in the suburbs. This was his stop, and he got off.

Jackie used the public phone to call the number on the paper, and soon saw a man without a shirt driving a motorbike, exposing the rolls of fat on his tummy; Beijing middle-aged men who casually tend to go shirtless in warmer weather are said to be wearing a "Beijing bikini." Unexpectedly, the Beijing bikini man stopped right in front of Jackie. "Are you Liu Peng? Then hop on!" So Jackie got on, loaded with two suitcases and three book bags strapped to his back.

He drove Jackie to a compound with red brick walls; Jackie saw many young people, some younger than he. A man led him to a single-story house. The living room had a TV and DVD player and several young men were watching a movie. Jackie entered another big room with more than thirty beds. After Jackie had chosen his bunk bed, he stored his luggage and rested on his bed.

After a while he heard people gathering and he followed them. In the house courtyard were about thirty men and a man was calling out names, including Jackie's. They formed an orderly line. Jackie was bewildered but the man next to him whispered, "We are going to shoot a movie." Jackie got excited, and followed the group.

As Jackie walked along, he looked at the gray city wall and

discovered a grand city gate tower familiar from the movies. He saw the name written over the main gate, Bayi Film Lot (八一影视基地, not to be confused with the similar-sounding Bayi Film Studio, where Jackie had auditioned earlier).

After Jackie entered the main gate, he saw rows of buildings used in the movies, streets, tea houses, a theater, hutongs and courtyard houses. Suddenly, he saw a tank. How exciting! He continued to follow the line; they passed through several streets and encountered Japanese soldiers. Actually, they were Chinese extras playing Japanese soldiers.

A man led Jackie and his group to a trailer and said, "Stand in line, take your costumes." Jackie's was a 长袍, or *changpao* (a traditional Chinese man's robe). They were going to shoot a war movie set several decades ago and Jackie was playing an ordinary man in the street. They filmed without a break until 11:00 p.m. After it was a wrap, Jackie put his own clothes back on, stood in line, and they returned to the compound. He lay on his bunk bed, chuckled, and thought to himself, "What fun!" Only that morning he had still been on the train to Beijing; that evening he had already started his acting career as an extra.

In the next several days, Jackie would play several roles, including a revolutionary soldier fighting for New China. His head was shaven. Several actors were placed in a row. Someone came over and asked Jackie, "Have you ever 'died' before?"

"What?" Jackie exclaimed.

"Do you know how to fall to the ground?" the crew member asked.

"Of course," Jackie replied, and he immediately fell backwards to the ground. He remembered how in the movies those who had been shot all fell to the ground, so he at once "drew a tiger while using a cat as a model" as he told me later, using the Chinese idiom 照猫画虎. That means he got it more or less right by doing a simple, rather crude imitation and falling to the ground.

When the crew member saw this, he was satisfied and said Jackie had done it fast. "Here is a bag of blood," he said. Inside that bag of fake blood was a wire. During filming, once it was activated remotely, it would explode and the blood would flow out naturally. That was the blood flow you see in movies and on TV once someone was shot. The crew member tucked the blood bag inside Jackie's clothes on the left side of his chest and told him not to touch it, and that once he heard gunshots to fall to the ground as he had just done and ignore everything else.

Once the cameras were rolling, Jackie remained fearless and focused. "As I was staring at the enemy, the comrade to my left burst into song and sang the first line of 'The Internationale.' I immediately joined in passionately singing the second line with seven other people."

"Then I heard a soldier yelling, 'Prepare, Shoot!' and the sound of gunfire. Suddenly, something exploded on the left side of my chest. I immediately fell to the ground. I remained motionless and heard an ear-splitting gunshot. My comrades had also fallen to the ground. 'Cut!' At that moment it started to rain, and it wasn't artificial rain; it was really raining!" he told me.

But not all days at the Bayi Film Lot were as exciting and action-packed. Some days Jackie wasn't called upon, which he found disappointing, so he spent the days with the other extras chatting, watching movies, reading books and newspapers or sleeping. The food was different on the days the actors were off. If you were shooting, they gave you a meal box with a drumstick, rice and vegetables; if you had to stay behind, you ate porridge, steamed buns and a bit of hot pickled mustard tuber.

"The people there were all like me, all had dreams, all liked movies and wanted to become movie stars," Jackie said. Moments of excitement alternated with disappointment when he wasn't called upon to film, and despite the valuable experience he was getting, he occasionally questioned whether he had made the right decision to come to Beijing. He stuck it out or a while.

Eventually, he was promoted to supervising the extras, bringing perks of better food and better living conditions—sharing sleeping quarters with only one other man, instead of thirty or more—yet Jackie was frustrated because he wasn't acting anymore. That, and the fact he was being paid almost nothing, led to his secretly packing his bags and stealing away from the Bayi Film Lot one night, after three months.

While he was sitting in the bus, Jackie thought about where he should go. He had a new ID card his mother had mailed to him and he had more than 100 yuan (roughly USD 14) in his pocket. While he was at the Bayi Film Lot, he had heard they were looking for extras at the Beijing Film Studio, so that was his next destination.

When Jackie finally arrived downtown at the Beijing Film Studio, which was located at the Beijing Film Academy in Haidian District, he felt very fresh. This was China's prestigious film school and Asia's largest! While he was standing at the roadside beside the gate of the Beijing Film Studio, he saw all kinds of people, some toting schoolbags or stools, elderly people, people with long or short hair, all kinds of people. These people were all looking for jobs.

After a while, someone asked Jackie, "Are you interested in filming? If so, pay me 30 yuan (a little less than USD 5) for transport." Jackie immediately agreed, because he had no place to stay that night. So all his luggage was loaded into a van, and Jackie and other extras were whisked away to their next gig. He played an Eighth Route Army soldier for two days, and he and the other extras marched at different speeds on a road, back and forth.

"Of course, I was happy as I didn't need to think about food and accommodation," he remembered. "The most important thing was to be alive." When the shooting was over, Jackie was paid 60 yuan (less than USD 10) for two days, then driven back to the gate of the Beijing Film Studio.

Jackie was now standing alone in front of the Beijing Film Studio gate. What should he do? Would someone ask him to act in a movie today? He had nowhere to stay and the Beijing winter was very cold. Fortunately, Jackie remembered a contact from the Bayi Film Lot, a man called Qin Bin (覃斌). When Jackie told Qin Bin he had a lot of luggage to store while looking for work, Qin Bin found a storage space and a place for Jackie to spend the night.

In the days to come, like many people dreaming of becoming successful actors, Jackie appeared at the gate of the Beijing Film Studio every morning at 6:00 a.m., waiting for opportunities. It was there he also found his first portrait modeling gig. The payment was 40 yuan (a little less than USD 6) per day. As Jackie is naturally curious, he agreed to be a portrait model for art students. He was asked to sit on a stool on a podium in front of the classroom. Only one requirement: Don't fall asleep!

"I was laughing inside," Jackie recalled. "I heard that models would fall asleep after working for a while. I didn't believe it then! But in the following days while working as a model, I did fall asleep sometimes." Of course, he was always promptly awakened by the students. After four hours of modeling, Jackie was paid and returned to the Beijing Film Studio. When he arrived at the gate, it was almost dark. Jackie was hungry. He didn't have the luxury of choosing a restaurant, because he didn't have a lot of money.

Jackie finally found a small Shanxi noodle restaurant with three migrant workers eating inside. There was a menu on the wall. Jackie ordered a bowl of tomato and egg noodles for 12 yuan (less than USD 2) and thought it was a little expensive, compared to noodles at home. He rarely ate out. Jackie was given free soup with the noodles and ended up drinking four bowls of soup. Again, where would he spend the night?

At the gate of the Beijing Film Studio a man suggested Jackie just go to a McDonald's because without spending money, you could sit there until 5:00 a.m. the next morning. After a while, Jackie found a McDonald's, picked a quiet place and sat down, without disturbing anyone. "I became tired and fell asleep at the table. In the middle of the night, I awoke and knew my body was telling me I couldn't sit here and sleep. But I didn't want to fall asleep in the cold wind, and I didn't have enough money to pay for a hotel room. Sitting inside McDonald's made me feel warm, and I hoped tomorrow would dawn early," Jackie remembered.

Others were doing the same thing. They washed their faces and brushed their teeth in the McDonald's restroom before going back to the gate of the Beijing Film Studio. It was early in the morning, but already there were all kinds of people at the gate looking for all kinds of unskilled jobs. Jackie hung out around the gate for more than a year. He went there in the mornings and left in the evenings; if he didn't land a gig, he went anyway. This was where his dream lay.

Jackie made friends with other aspiring actors at the gate. They told him that if he wanted to land roles, he must make a resume with his photos and audition with film crews. He distributed his resume, sometimes going to four different places in a day to submit them, but no one contacted him.

After spending a long time without a bath, he would shower in a public bath near a university, which was cheap. When he wasn't staying overnight in a McDonald's or KFC, he would go to a nearby public toilet in the morning to wash his face. When his hair was really too dirty, or smelled really awful, he would wash it with free hand soap in a public toilet. He would charge his phone at internet cafés, where he sometimes spent the night. Worst case scenarios found Jackie spending the night in public toilets. He would eat a bowl of noodles and drink several bowls of free soup at the Shanxi noodle restaurant. If he was filming, he had his meals with the crew, of course, for free. This was how Jackie lived in Beijing.

During his first winter in Beijing, and after submitting his resume a hundred times, Jackie landed only one acting gig. But it would prove to be a very intriguing opportunity.

One day Jackie went to an audition with his friend Qin Bin. When they arrived, a group of actors was already there waiting. Soon someone shouted and asked them to stand straight, as the director was about to select actors. Jackie saw a man in his fifties stroll out of a room and walk in front of them. He looked at the actors for less than eight seconds and then they were suddenly told to leave. Jackie's temper exploded. This was it?! Weren't they supposed to audition individually? He and Qin Bin had come for the audition in the freezing cold winter and it cost them four yuan (USD 0.60) each in bus fare.

Jackie whispered to Qin Bin that they wouldn't leave. Qin Bin was confused, but Jackie told him to follow him and they hid in the restroom, where they changed into suits. They would try to audition again. The two friends changed their clothes, slicked back their hair with tap water and polished their leather shoes. When they arrived at the director's room, they decided Jackie should go first, so he entered as the door was open. There was a man inside, the same man who had previously told them all to leave. He was sitting on a sofa, looking at actors' resumes.

"Haven't you been here already?" he asked, visibly annoyed. Jackie took a step back and stood with his chest out and asked him how he had performed. "Go out and wait!" the man said loudly and Jackie left. Then, Qin Bin went in. After a while he also came out. When Jackie asked him how it had gone, he didn't answer. Jackie said he would wait a little longer, but Qin Bin had had enough of this adventure and decided to leave.

Jackie waited, and it grew dark outside. Suddenly the director came out and snapped, "You're still here?" Oh! Jackie understood that meant he had been chosen and he should go down to the lobby. He was so happy! Jackie got into a minibus with several others. After a roll call, the bus took off. Two hours passed and they arrived at a hotel, where Jackie was put into a room with a fellow actor. They were all told to assemble at the hotel entrance at 6:00 a.m. the next morning. "If you don't show up, don't come again," the team leader said.

The next morning, they were driven to the Zhuozhou Film and Television Studio (河北涿州影视城) in Hebei, the province bordering Beijing. They entered a large film studio with a few rooms inside, streets, halls, bedrooms and podiums. Jackie was given a white outfit and a white cap and only when the cameras started rolling did Jackie realize he was playing a cook extra in the 2011 movie *The 1911 Revolution* (辛亥革命), a movie that would be released on the centennial of the historic event that saw the establishment of the Republic of China after the Qing dynasty (AD 1644 - AD 1911) was overthrown.

As Jackie was taking a break from filming, he asked another actor, "Who is the star?"

"Why, it's Jackie Chan," the actor replied.

My Jackie couldn't believe it. "You got to be kidding!" he exclaimed. What he couldn't believe was that, as a big Jackie Chan fan, he could meet his idol and be part of his movie.

Suddenly, he saw Jackie Chan enter, wearing a military uniform and cap. There were staff around him. "My heart was pounding. I stood up, and walked toward him. But my feet were so heavy that I couldn't lift them. My idol! I was very excited that after watching his movies for more than ten years, I was now seeing Jackie Chan," my Jackie recalled.

On the second day of shooting, Jackie Chan approached my Jackie and asked him if he had eaten yet.

"No," he replied loudly and Jackie Chan turned away and fetched a big loaf of bread for my Jackie. The superstar then opened another bread bag, tore off a piece and popped it into his own mouth.

"Neither have I!" said Jackie Chan.

Another tip Jackie learned at the gate of Beijing Film Studio was that if he was chosen as a supporting actor, he would travel with the film crew for several months, live and eat with them, and thus didn't have to spend money on housing and food. He landed such an opportunity with the 2013 TV series *The Legend of Hua Mulan* (花木兰传奇), which took Jackie to Jiangsu province and Inner Mongolia. Another example was Jackie's playing a kind-hearted army captain in the Eighth Route Army called Captain Liu, who is tricked by opium smugglers and killed in the 2012 war drama *Northwest Wolf in Warfare* (战火西北狼). Filming took place in Jackie's native Shaanxi province and Beijing over several months, and he had some lines. Usually, Jackie would go on to play mostly "good guys," but one TV series several years later would see him out of character playing a bad guy. Ironically, I think Jackie playing a bad guy was one of his most convincing performances. Jackie then admitted it was hard to hit his opponent in one scene, although he didn't actually have to hit, just strike out and pretend.

When Jackie returned to Beijing after filming *The Legend of*

Hua Mulan, his friend Qin Bin helped arrange new lodgings: a shared room in a residential compound apartment with five other people in Wangjing, where Jackie was living when I first met him in 2012. Each night cost 15 yuan (USD 2) and each shower 1.5 yuan (roughly USD 0.20). The landlord, Mr. Li, kindly introduced Jackie to modeling gigs at art institutions.

In Wangjing, in addition to working as an actor and model, Jackie also found two part-time jobs: He worked in a Korean restaurant, introducing the dishes to guests, and in a golf stadium, receiving the players and retrieving golf balls.

"I would starve to death by only doing films, because I could not film every day, nor could I earn that much money," Jackie admitted. At one point in Beijing, he also sold small household items displayed on a blanket on the sidewalk.

In 2014, Jackie spent the Spring Festival at his home in Yang County. When he learned they were recruiting actors for the 2015 TV series *The Chinese Farmers* (老农民, literally, *Old Farmers*), he applied.

"My father is a farmer and I am the child of a farmer," Jackie recalled. "I was very touched by the sentiments of ordinary people and farmers. Also, the TV series had such a good cast, director and actors, I was really attracted by it."

He was selected as a supporting actor. When Jackie told his father the good news that he was going to Shandong province to shoot *The Chinese Farmers*, his father was skeptical. "You aren't married yet! How can you act as an 'old farmer'?" his father asked in disbelief.

Anyhow, Jackie joined the crew in a small stone village in Shandong for five months as an "old farmer," and he learned a lot about agricultural tools used by the local people, for example, cutting wheat, hoeing the ground, sowing seeds, growing tobacco, and how farmers walk and squat.

HUTONG HEARTTHROBS

One day, a crew member from Henan told Jackie, "Look, there is recruitment information for a stand-in actor. The height and body shape are similar to yours. Would you like to try?" Jackie wasn't interested at first. A few weeks later, the Henan fellow told Jackie that they were still looking for a stand-in. Jackie had a different mindset this time — in several days, they would wrap up filming *The Chinese Farmers*, and he would be out of work. So this time, Jackie applied for the stand-in role.

He was asked to interview — in Beijing. So Jackie traveled from Shandong to China's capital. When Jackie arrived at the hotel for the interview, the casting director looked him up and down and said they would take a few photos of Jackie from the front and back. Then he was asked to read several lines. Afterwards, the casting director unexpectedly asked Jackie to go to the hotel rooftop with him.

"He wanted me perform kung fu," Jackie told me. The casting director set up a camera and said, "What can you do? Let's start!" So Jackie performed a set of boxing punches he had learned as a soldier in Sichuan. After he was done, the casting director asked, "What else can you do?" Jackie performed his favorite tai chi moves a few times, before the casting director asked him again, "What else?" Jackie finally uttered the rather ridiculous line, inspired by Jackie Chan's 2012 movie *Chinese Zodiac* (十二生肖) in which Jackie Chan is being chased by Doberman Pinschers: "French dogs speak Chinese, and I am playing the role of a dog again, woof, woof, woof!" Then, he did push-ups.

When Jackie told me about this audition, I thought, what an unusual job interview; I got an adrenaline rush just hearing about it. He told me he had already suspected it was a stand-in role for Jackie Chan, which was confirmed by the agent before the audition, so he had prepared very carefully. After the audition, Jackie was told to wait for a reply, so he returned to Yang County, where he worked on his physical fitness in the hopes that he would be chosen. Soon he received a call with the stunning news that he had been indeed chosen as a stand-in for Jackie Chan in the 2016 movie *Skiptrace* (绝地逃亡). For that movie, he worked with Jackie Chan for four months in Inner Mongolia, Beijing and Guangxi.

"Every beginning is difficult," Jackie admitted, teaching me a popular Chinese saying (万事开头难). He was even familiar with the English phrase, "Rome wasn't built in a day," which he repeated to me in his heavily accented English in the same context of telling me how he began his life in Beijing and broke into the acting industry.

This was my Jackie's life up until that May day when he encountered me in the subway in 2012, and beyond when I returned to Beijing in 2015. To me, such a life as Jackie's was hard to imagine.

4

Homecoming

While I was working in San Francisco, during the first couple of months after my return to the US in 2012, I missed China a lot. For a long time, I was still in Beijing in my thoughts, you could even say still on "Beijing time," because I would check the time and temperature there on my new smart phone several times a day (however, I still had the mobile phone I had used in Beijing to communicate with Jackie with my Chinese SIM card in it; it was carefully tucked away in a drawer together with some memories). I felt strangely displaced in a way.

TAMMY TREICHEL

The company I was working for was located right next to the picturesque Bayside. During my lunch break, I took walks next to the water and watched airplanes taking off from the San Francisco airport, thinking of my friends in China and pinning my best wishes to the tails of the planes, including for Jackie. I remember feeling a lack of enthusiasm to acclimate myself to my new environment, despite its beautiful scenery, pleasant Mediterranean climate, and the cool, laid-back attitude of Californians. I then moved to Houston and made a feeble attempt to become a token Texas girl but failed. Maybe I was lazy, maybe I was depressed... Maybe I missed Jackie?

My friend Beixi, who by then had left Beijing and returned to her native Singapore, told me in an email, "Tamara, sometimes Beijing felt like one very long, very colorful dream." Come to think of it, I longed for it; it was such an exciting and dynamic place despite the smog, spittle on the streets and high cultural barriers.

During that period, Jackie emailed me photos of our old neighborhood in Wangjing and then of his acting stints all over China, including one of himself with an ostrich and another of him with lamas, and even an audio recording wishing me well. In the background of the audio recording, I could hear the sounds of Beijing, the hustle and bustle of the big city and car motors.

My job in San Francisco was not very exciting; I was chained to my office desk for eight hours a day, Monday through Friday. But vicariously, through Jackie, who went to different places and had different encounters every day due to his work, I could lead a more interesting life. "I am your legs," Jackie once told me. I liked his metaphorical thinking!

"Guard your heart," my new San Francisco friend and housemate Regina told me. "Everything that you do flows from it." She was a world-wise woman who had experienced a lot of turbulence in life and knew what she was talking about.

This was the complete opposite of the "open your heart" advice I had received from my Chinese ex-boyfriend in Heidelberg. I think the truth lies somewhere in between: You should open your heart to the right people, places and experiences after careful deliberation. And upon reflecting on this for a long, long time, I decided to seek out Jackie and Beijing again. It was not an impulsive decision and required a lot of thought and planning, but all along, I was acting from the bottom of my heart.

Three long years after leaving China and several jobs and many adventures later, there was a job vacancy at my former workplace in Beijing, and I was able to return to China after a long wait for my work visa. When I arrived, it was like a homecoming. I could barely suppress my excitement as I once again spotted the armies of poplar trees on the outskirts of Beijing outside the taxi window upon leaving the airport. I felt like the poplars were my welcoming committee.

When I returned to Beijing for my second stint in China, a coworker taught me the Chinese proverb, "A crafty rabbit has three burrows" (狡兔三窟) – in my case, that would be the US, Germany and now China. That same coworker also once asked me at lunch in the canteen, "Tammy, do you pray before a meal?"

"Sometimes," I replied rather shyly. I went on to tell her I was in search of a "home" – geographically and spiritually.

"Home is where the love is," this coworker replied simply. I understood that to mean "home is where the heart is." I nodded. And several years later I would come to realize my home was with Jackie, as that was where my heart lay. Rather amusingly, someone would later refer to this story of mine as being similar to the Julia Roberts film *Eat, Pray, Love* – although I must concede that there is less "eating" and "praying" going on here.

TAMMY TREICHEL

Most of the time in China, I wasn't American or for that matter, German (I have dual citizenship) but simply a "foreigner." I would come to revel in that role as many Chinese were not that familiar with foreign ways and had few expectations about how a foreigner should or shouldn't behave. Meanwhile, Jackie just accepts and embraces me for who I am.

While in Beijing, I would try to make use of almost every opportunity to mix with the Chinese as I got more comfortable interacting with them and my language skills improved. After all, one of my coworkers had told me, "Every Chinese person is a window." I loved that metaphor and when I told one of my other coworkers the very same thing, he laughed merrily and said, "We have too many windows!" Yes, over one billion of them... I did have time to peek into quite a few. Good local friends were windows with beautiful curtains always drawn aside for me, and Jackie would prove not only to be a window, but also a big, elaborately carved door. I was so grateful to those Chinese who opened their hearts and homes to me.

"I noticed here I am more spontaneous, less set in my ways, less averse to changes, freer to bestow praise, love and kindness on others," read a rather upbeat journal entry from my first days in China during the 2009-2012 period.

Upon my return to Beijing, I went apartment hunting by myself as I could more or less get around using Chinese now. I even reconnected with a leasing agent I had met during my first stint in China. His telephone number was stored on my old flip phone that also contained Jackie's number—both still worked. I was really surprised that despite the dynamic changes in Beijing, a lot actually remained unchanged since I had left in 2012.

During my first strolls upon my return, I saw a man on a motorcycle. In front of him, wedged between his chest and the handlebars, was his passenger: a dog wearing sunglasses. Yes, I was back in Beijing, the "eternal city" of the East.

For me, things would get both progressively easier but also harder, and definitely not less intriguing after my first three years as I delved deeper into culture and society. It got easier in the sense that Jackie would later join me as a companion and guide, but harder as I realized how really complex it could be to navigate local society, so I resigned myself to my limitations. Some things I had found interesting or charming at the beginning gradually lost their luster and became part of my daily experience or even downright annoying; then again there were new things I was discovering that really excited me. But of course, every expat has his or her own China journey.

In 2015, I thought I had "graduated" in terms of Beijing life and could now try living in a hutong house and get a feeling for the fabled hutong culture. During my first stint in China, I moved to Wangjing, where I had my first open shower, i.e., a shower without a stall just enclosed by a curtain. Now, I thought I was hardened enough to live with a "shoilet" if necessary—a shower nozzle directly above the toilet, with no stall and no curtain. The leftover water would be pushed towards the drain using a mop, and you wore plastic slippers every time you entered the bathroom immediately after a shower. Finding a decent shower and shower stall, Western-style, usually required a high budget in Beijing now, so a "shoilet" seemed the more frugal way to go.

I finally found the perfect place, a bungalow in one of Beijing's classic areas, not far from the Yonghegong Lama Temple (雍和宫) and Guozijian (国子监), the latter being the Beijing Confucian Temple and Imperial College complex. Jackie would join me soon in my new hutong house.

Hutong houses are popular among some more seasoned Beijing expats, and they can be rather old, Spartan-like and plainly furnished or completely refurbished and stylishly decorated (and thus a lot more expensive to rent). Hutongs are narrow alleys that date back several centuries to the Yuan dynasty (AD 1271 - AD 1368), when Beijing was also the capital. Recently many hutong houses have been torn down to make way for roads and high-rises — you can recognize the "writing on the wall" for some doomed buildings as the character 拆 (*chai*, or "tear down") is scrawled on them.

With various leasing agents, I toured several hutong houses in northeast Beijing, but there were none I fell in love with.

After two agents had shown me all they had to offer in the way of hutong houses, I met with Tonny (yes, "Tonny" with a double "n"). Chinese occasionally go for variations on conventional English names or adopt rather avant-garde ones like "Castle" or "Seven." Tonny was the leasing agent whose number I had already stored on my old mobile phone as he must have shown me some apartments during my first stint in Beijing. After reconnecting with him, I hopped on the back of his scooter.

Tonny drove me to a hutong house hidden in a maze of narrow lanes, not far away from the famous Yonghegong Lama Temple. As his scooter snaked through the lanes, I noticed the pungent smell of incense, reminding me the gods were not far away.

We stopped in front of a strong metal door. An elderly couple stood on the door stoop, smiling at me. They beckoned to me to enter.

I came, saw, and was conquered.

"The apartment has its own tiny courtyard where you can dry your clothes and a living room and bedroom with sufficient furniture. The bathroom and kitchen are private (in some hutongs you share them with neighbors), and the apartment has a southern exposure, so it is sunny," I gushed in an email to my mother, attaching photos.

But I would not be going in blind and "buying a pig in a poke" in China! After inspecting the hutong house carefully, I sat down to talk to the landlord and his wife, who sat on one of the chairs like a prim lady in a Qing-dynasty painting.

The couple made a very positive impression — a good landlord is as important as a good apartment; after all, they come as a package.

The conversation was all in Chinese as neither the couple nor Tonny could speak English, so this is what I understood from my limited command of Chinese. The Chinese parties were very considerate and spoke more slowly for me so I would have an easier time understanding them. The landlord said his family had lived in the house for generations; they used to keep dogs, rabbits and pigeons in the small courtyard. The neighborhood used to be quite lively with many vendors selling their goods and people used to stand in line to receive blessings (a touch on the head) from lamas. Also, the Imperial Academy where the emperor used to select and approve the essays of renowned scholars was practically next door, and next to the Imperial Academy was the Confucius Temple, which made a lot of sense as Confucius was long regarded as China's top sage.

Friendly landlords, a cozy hutong house in one of China's most culturally and historically rich neighborhoods, plus stories to go with it. Could it get any better?

I made a quick mental review of the apartment and found only one problem, which might prove to be my Waterloo.

There was no toilet in the bathroom!

I pointed out the problem to Tonny and the landlord.

"No toilet, no contract," I said vehemently in my rather heavily accented Chinese.

Tonny told me with a serious mien that he knew a young

TAMMY TREICHEL

American expat, a hutong dweller, who didn't need his own toilet and liked to use the public restrooms across the street as a way to connect with his Chinese neighbors and improve his Chinese. Oh no, no. No way!

However, the landlord said they could easily install a new toilet and pointed to a hole in the ground in the bathroom. I liked the rest of the apartment so after giving the matter a lot of consideration — taking into account the house's charm and proximity to public transportation and supermarkets, famous bar and food streets convenient for meeting friends, as well as Chinese cultural and historical sites — I finally agreed to rent it. I gave Tonny a small deposit to secure the apartment, but insisted on seeing the newly installed toilet before signing the contract.

The next few days, the toilet issue was constantly on my mind, but Tonny assured me the plumbing was already set up. Several days later, the landlord led me to the bathroom and presented a shiny new Western-style toilet, or "porcelain throne." When I said in Chinese I wanted to "try the toilet out," the landlord and Tonny were visibly nervous — actually, I meant "flush it," not actually use it yet — so the landlord gently flushed the toilet, careful not to disturb the drying caulk.

The toilet had a special lid, as the shower head was almost directly above the toilet — the notorious "shoilet" expats tend to complain about. The special lid keeps the toilet dry after you take a shower. Actually, when you think about it, the shoilet is a simple, yet clever solution because it saves a lot of space and materials. When our toilet was replaced four years later, the new toilet had an apple-shaped sticker on its lid that read "iPhoade," which was obviously evocative of "iPhone" and meant to vouch for the toilet's quality. (Jackie joked that we had been upgraded to an Apple-brand toilet.)

But back to the original toilet in the hutong house. I had to take a leap of faith and flush down my doubts. It worked.

Upon moving into the hutong house, I noticed the landlord and his wife had hung new curtains in the bedroom. The kitchen was now stocked with dishes and utensils, including a rusty kitchen knife. Well, I had had a tetanus shot recently. For reasons of safety and/or simply because I didn't know where to look, I discovered that buying knives in Beijing was like a quest for the Holy Grail. In Walmart I was told China was a "safe country" and that they didn't carry any knives, so a coworker would later give me one of her spares. This was before I could navigate the wonders of the e-commerce platform Taobao, which has an inexhaustible amount of goods, including knives.

Speaking of knives, occasionally the knife-sharpener, a relic of another age, would pass by our hutong with his whetstone on a cart, calling out for customers. Jackie was delighted and sometimes rushed out to get a blade sharpened or buy flour from the itinerant flour and cooking oil vendor. To him, they were not relics but reminders of his boyhood near Xi'an.

In the hutong house, there was now a Terracotta Warrior figure on the dining room table, a stuffed gorilla on the sofa and bifocals and playing cards on a dresser. And, oh joy! There was also a new pink toilet brush, which the landlord had ceremoniously placed next to the newly installed toilet.

Now the landlord and his wife had done their part, and they expected me to do mine. On the back of a piece of cardboard torn from a box of Double Happiness tobacco, the landlord had left meticulously written instructions in Chinese—I needed to open the drain in my courtyard, which was usually covered by a lid, to divert the rainwater in the summer to avoid flooding, and sweep away the leaves in the autumn because they posed a fire hazard.

When I proudly told a coworker I had moved into my very own courtyard house, or 四合院 (*siheyuan*), he jokingly remarked,

"You are a rich woman." But another coworker who had helped me move my luggage corrected me quickly by saying it wasn't technically a *siheyuan* as I didn't share a courtyard with others. Still, my pride wasn't diminished. It was a hutong house, a bungalow, with a small, private courtyard.

By and large, I have been a happy camper ever since, although there were and are minor annoyances, or, to give them a more positive spin, "China challenges."

My electricity boxes, where you can check how many kilowatt-hours you still have left after purchasing some electricity, are located in the neighbor's courtyard. I have two electricity boxes, one for the bedroom and one for the living room, kitchen and bathroom area. The landlord had forgotten to show me where my electricity boxes were so I asked a neighbor to help with what I thought would be a straightforward task. That evening, when I answered the door, a whole group of neighbors was standing on my door stoop. They were curious about their new foreign neighbor and wanted to check me out. Together with my welcoming committee, after several failed detours, we found the boxes in my next door neighbor's hallway. Life in China complicated? Tell me about it!

What's more, I had to learn to be patient and wait to take a hot shower as I needed to turn on the boiler first. This made me enjoy my hot showers even more. I had been told that living in a hutong would be quiet, but mine appeared to be an exception, except in winter, when people stayed indoors. Mornings found me eavesdropping on retirees chewing the fat at my door stoop. Moreover, a community center is just a stone's throw away, contributing to pedestrian traffic and making me feel I always need to be on my best behavior.

Finally, when I came home from work in the warmer months, I sometimes had to dodge a soccer ball being kicked around by neighborhood kids, which quickly corrected my initial impression of Chinese children dividing their lives between their schools and homes, studying all the time. And there was a very well-maintained rooster that liked to strut his stuff near the garbage cans and squawk—someone's pet, or future dinner—that lent a countryside touch to my city life. To my delight, there were also occasional house lizards, adults and babies in the niches of my little courtyard. According to popular belief, a lizard in the home is a sign of good luck, and of course, they eat pesky insects.

Once Jackie returned to Beijing and moved in with me into the hutong abode not too long after I had rented it in 2015, the little hutong house, its concomitant responsibilities, pet lizards and the impressions it left naturally all became "our" Villa Villekulla (house of Pippi Longstocking, the colorful Swedish fictional character), not just mine.

We had a baby lizard, the offspring of our two adults. I made a little covered nest for the lizards in the courtyard and left a saucer of water for the baby. "Thank you very much," Jackie told me in English, then added in Chinese "for helping China," in reference to the rescue of our little guest. I was tickled by Jackie's humorous reaction.

Jackie and I have had a lot of fun with the nature surrounding our hutong house—be it watching a woodpecker hammering away at the huge poplar tree next to our home, or making a bird feeder out of a big plastic water bottle and hanging it in our little yard. I filled it with sunflower seeds, but alas, no birds came. But not to worry, when I peeked out of the kitchen window, I found a rather strange "Big Bird" visiting the feeder: Jackie was helping himself to the seeds; many Chinese like to snack on sunflower seeds. Remember, the fabled roc flies ten thousand miles (*li*) to success.

All in all, the hutong house, Jackie and I are a match made in heaven. For us, living in the little old hutong house in downtown Beijing is like living in an Impressionistic painting.

I loved to open the kitchen door and let sunlight stream in during the late afternoon, and I loved the wind rustling through the poplar trees next to our home. There were weeds growing among the roof shingles, and I liked to watch the wind tousle the weeds. I loved our own personal patch of Beijing blue sky—at least without the notorious air pollution. At night, the hutong roofs served as catwalks for felines to hunt for mates, and I made a sport of watching them while lying in bed. On occasion, the sky was freckled with stars and the moon rose and descended behind the shingles. Most of all, I was impressed by that clever invention, the shoilet, but Jackie preferred the public squat toilets in our neighborhood because he grew up with them.

I consider myself fortunate to still be able to experience the "hutong culture" as hutong houses are slowly becoming a thing of the past. In fifty years, there will be fewer opportunities to live and breathe Beijing history in a hutong house, although there will always be some for preservation purposes and tourists.

My experience has been worth the minor annoyances. It has been like living in a historic bed-and-breakfast every day squat in the heart of Beijing, only meters away from the Imperial Academy and the Confucius and Yonghegong Lama temples, and only several subway stops from the Forbidden City. I have loved (almost) every minute of my stay in our high-maintenance hutong house, and I trust the same could be said of Jackie.

But winter in a hutong house has its challenges. The houses are colder than standard apartments as they are not well insulated. Hutong inhabitants don't get the government-subsidized heat for Beijing's high-rises, meaning you have to pay for electricity to heat yourself. An American coworker said it gets so cold you don't have to refrigerate your beer, and he quickly moved out of his hutong.

Yet it has been toasty in our hutong house due to the heaters in the living room, kitchen and bedroom and an additional heater-air conditioner. We also have two extra space heaters on standby.

As we leap from autumn into winter, a tidal wave of leaves breaks over our little courtyard. The leaves come from a poplar tree that gives us a lot of pleasure with its rustling in the summer. Early one morning in November, Jackie and I woke up from a pitter-patter sound. I said, "We need to take in the laundry! It's raining!" A wide-eyed Jackie rushed to the window: Indeed, it was "raining," but it wasn't water, it was leaves! "It's like in the countryside," Jackie observed, and I could sense his contentment. After all, he is still a country boy at heart.

Still, I admired the beauty of "our" poplar tree with its lush summer green and brittle, autumn green-gold mottled leaves. The transition of seasons doesn't occur gradually in Beijing; it's a sudden change, a jolt that leaves little time for poetic musings. The leaves don't even have time to fully turn gold before they are yanked from the trees. And then comes the bitter Beijing cold.

Ah, the Beijing winter. The neighborhood was a lot more silent, and the silence was only occasionally interrupted by the wailing of a child. It was a church-like silence at times, with no chickens clucking or children playing. There were fewer cat sightings in our hutong "hood" as well. The house lizards were gone, so were the chickens — all hibernating, indoors or eaten.

At least, there are no heavy rains in Beijing in winter. The flash floods in summer once caused a Titanic-like flood in our kitchen as the drainage in the little courtyard is poor and the kitchen door flimsy, with Jackie helping me shovel out the ankle-deep water. Since then, we have always been leaving the drain in the courtyard uncovered to divert the rainwater; even if it started to pour and we weren't at home, there was nothing to worry about.

TAMMY TREICHEL

Hutong houses stand out in their stark naked beauty in winter. Winter is the time to admire the designs on the roof tiles, for example the jade rabbit from Chinese mythology that is pounding the elixir of immortality but looks as if it is actually mopping the floor. I discovered another tile that depicted a rider bearing down on his horse and a series of tiles that featured a traditional Chinese knot which I jokingly referred to as "China Unicom (中国联通) tiles." Unicom is one of China's biggest telecommunications provider and its emblem is a similar knot.

Winter is also the time to contemplate the inner beauty of hutong houses, the plaster flaking off the moist walls and take in their musty smell. In some ways, Beijing is like Rome — an "eternal city" — yet in some ways it isn't, sadly, with environmental factors and human activities chipping away at its relics. Here today, gone tomorrow. Beijing's hutongs are a good case in point.

If you rent an apartment in Beijing, you also rent the landlord and/or landlady. It is somewhat like getting "married," so it is important you find a good match because you have to deal with them in the long term. For me, it was love at first — or at least second — sight with the elderly couple who own our hutong house.

Chinese people talk about *yuanfen* (缘分), which means a chance encounter or fate that brings and binds people together. Before I met my current landlord couple, I thought the concept of *yuanfen* was overrated. A prospective landlady who liked me and wanted me to move into an apartment she was renting out had used the term in reference to me when I was leaving Liufang in 2011. Yet when she wanted one year's rent up front, a request I found unreasonable, I did not think we had *yuanfen* at all and that was the end of our interactions. But next to my first encounter with Jackie, it was this lovely elderly landlord couple that made me less skeptical about the concept. They have accommodated my every need and in return, I have carefully heeded their instructions on how to take care of the hutong house.

Just like me, the landlord couple appreciate classic cultural touches in their living space, along with a fusion of East and West, reflected beautifully in how "our" apartment was decorated. The Terracotta Warrior figurine standing proudly on the dining table, a plaster Venus de Milo gazing off into the distance from on top of the fridge. A tape I found in a drawer containing sweet, sentimental ballads from the Taiwanese singer Teresa Teng (also known as Deng Lijun, 邓丽君) later confirmed that my landlords and I shared certain tastes in music and were thus compatible. Jackie for his part was intrigued by a makeup kit from the Beijing Film Academy we found on the bookcase in the hall, complete with a fake mustache, which he promptly tried on.

Jackie and I and the landlord couple have become accustomed to visiting each other. The couple's apartment—they now live in a high-rise—is lovingly decorated, boasting a recent wedding photo of them taken in bridal wear because they didn't have the opportunity to take wedding photos when they were young. The landlord likes to smoke and sip tea, while the landlady takes great pride in her elegant appearance. I thought the landlady had beautiful teeth until she once took out her dentures to show them to me—our relationship had indeed reached the next level!

After several years, I dare say they treat me a bit like a surrogate daughter, despite their having two grown sons, one of them close by. They gave me gifts of tea or clothes, and I brought them souvenirs from my trips with Jackie. When Jackie had time, he joined us, and during one visit while I enjoyed listening to the landlord's account of the excavation of a Ming tomb, Jackie was fascinated by a yellow teddy bear on their couch. When Jackie told the landlady over a meal that her husband had been a dashing youth after seeing the landlord in a photo as a young man, she was visibly pleased.

We never have had any friction with the landlord and his wife, and they generally never complained about repairs in our high-maintenance hutong house. When we had a big roof leak in 2021 due to a rainy summer, which stained some of Jackie's acting costumes as well as the ceiling of the entrance hall and a living room wall, the landlord, Jackie and I worked together to find suitable repairmen, and Jackie supervised the roof repairs, sending the landlord photos via smart phone, while I was at work. Later, the landlord and his wife came over to inspect the results of the repair work in person, and after everything was deemed satisfactory, we sat down together and chatted amicably over tea.

What's more, in all the years since we have moved in, the landlord and his wife have only raised the rent once, and then in a very discreet fashion. "May we raise the rent?" the landlord asked me on that occasion. We quickly agreed upon a tiny amount. From what I could glean from our conversations, he and his wife wanted caring and orderly tenants and Jackie and I seem to fit the bill. A match made in heaven, indeed.

5

A HEALING TOUCH

The first one or two years upon returning to Beijing weren't that easy for me as I was grieving the loss of my father. A lot of suffering comes from the inability to accept change and "go with the flow."

Jackie and I had been in touch from time to time while I was in the US. On the night before my 35th birthday, I dreamed that Jackie had sought me out in San Francisco. "I just followed the road West from China," he told me. It was a very humorous and happy dream and when I woke up, I felt very refreshed.

TAMMY TREICHEL

"If you are happy, I am happy," he emailed me once during that time.

Outsiders called our relationship a "lovely fantasy," a "doomed romance," "wisps of smoke" and definitely a "low possibility event." A friend who meant well said, "Enjoy it while it lasts," which to me was indicative of today's ultra-realistic, rather cynical zeitgeist.

But they had all underrated the depth of our feelings for each other.

Jackie and I were reunited after three years apart on a sunny spring day, right under the eaves of the Yonghegong Lama Temple. He had been at home in Yang County in Shaanxi province for a while, and after my return to China, he made the long train journey from his hometown to Beijing to start a new life with me. When I first set eyes upon Jackie, he had sweat on his brow and was carrying a huge military-style backpack with a good luck charm featuring the twelve Chinese zodiac signs dangling from it. The first thing he would do when entering the hutong house was hang the charm in a window.

I took off my bug-eye sunglasses so I could see him clearly. Oh, there were the warm, chocolate-colored eyes and the crow's feet I liked so much when he smiled, and there were that familiar warm voice, and the small, calloused hands!

During the first one or two minutes, we were both a bit shy around each other, but quickly fell into a very natural and comfortable conversation. It was as though we had left off three hours ago; actually, we were where we had left off three years ago. I sought Jackie out very much like a moth, flying in the dark, instinctively seeks the light. His hand sought mine and we crossed the street in the direction of the hutong house. It felt right.

From what Jackie told me later on while sitting in the hutong house, he had experienced many mostly positive adventures in my absence and showed me a lot of photos on his phone. "My life is a movie!" he said, beaming.

Meanwhile, my US life had been more like a ridiculous reality show in which I was unwillingly cast rather than an exciting, fast-paced Hollywood movie with a happy ending. My father's cancer ordeal had left me broken and sad, but Jackie with his sunny personality handed me a flashlight as I crawled through a very dark tunnel.

What's more, the hutongs proved to be the perfect place to start my healing process. We live in a rather spiritual place, with the Yonghegong Lama Temple as the focal point of our neighborhood. Our landlord for his part subscribed to the popular belief that the *feng shui* (geomancy, energy flow) in the neighborhood was good.

It was only natural that in Yonghegong, the original meaning of which is "Palace of Harmony and Peace," Jackie and I would sooner or later chance upon thangkas (唐卡), which are Tibetan Buddhist paintings of a deity or scene that are either used for personal meditation or to instruct others.

I first heard of thangkas when I moved into our neighborhood. I would say the more obvious characteristics of our immediate neighborhood before you reach the Imperial Academy and Confucius Temple are the smell of incense from the Yonghegong Lama Temple, wafting through the hutongs, and occasional recorded announcements warning citizens not to be cheated by the fortune tellers. And of course, thangkas.

Next to some shops actually selling thangkas, you can see young men crouching, painting thangkas stretched on canvases, and that is what first got me interested. My first (and to date last) hands-on experience with thangkas was in the winter of 2015/2016, when I was going through the first Christmas without my father. Plus the winter months can be hard on the psyche, due to the lack of sunlight and the harsh Siberian winds. Winters in Beijing are like living in a black-and-white silent movie at times.

I discovered a thangka workshop in a hutong near our home, which was a godsend. The staff — a woman from northeast China and an elderly man who liked to smoke as well as a cat that liked to cozy up to customers — provided a haven for me in those months when I badly needed diversion. Creating a "Guanyin Pusa" thangka became my personal mission for about two months, and I visited the workshop more or less daily for short sessions, with Jackie looking in as well. It was good exercise in terms of self-discipline and concentration. Thangka art has been practiced for more than one thousand years; it is part of Himalayan cultural heritage. The thangka-making process has been described as "the spiritual cultivation of the creator."

Guanyin is the goddess of mercy and compassion in Chinese Buddhism. I thought this very suitable, as I had been given a second chance to come to China and start over with Jackie, in a way. In my painting, Guanyin is shown as a woman, in a white robe with legs crossed sitting on a lotus flower; she looks down demurely, holding a water flask in her left hand and a willow branch in her right. She was a figure a non-Buddhist such as I could easily relate to not only because of her anthropomorphic appearance, but because compassion and mercy are universal values. Plus, looking at my painting gave me a sense of temporary peace; to me, she was a sort of Asian "Mother Mary."

There are different kinds of thangkas, some are painted directly onto a canvas, and others, like the ones we created in the workshop, are created on a wooden board with glue, metal strips and a colored paste. You can deviate from the standard palette of your chosen pattern. For example, I made my sky a romantic cotton-candy pink, which was Jackie's idea. I decided my Guanyin would have brown, not black hair (after all, it was a foreign Guanyin). I could sense my teacher had reservations about the artistic choices of her renegade thangka student but she did not interfere.

On February 27, 2016, I completed my thangka and my teacher rather diplomatically said my work was not too bad, considering I was a foreigner and it was my first thangka. My Guanyin thangka is now in our hutong house, sitting high up on a cabinet, watching over Jackie and me. From far away, she looks perfect, but if you look closely, you will see blemishes. But perfection can lie in the eyes of the beholder, just like beauty.

Working on my Guanyin Pusa with Jackie was, from start to finish, a labor of love and healing. After all, it was about the journey, not the destination. I felt as if Guanyin had really heard my cries.

6

"I THOUGHT YOU SAID YOU LIKED CHALLENGES!"

"Thank *you* for giving me a home," Jackie told me upon joining me in the hutong house. "Thank you for giving me a home," I replied, thanking HIM for giving me a home in his heart. Coming home to the hutong house wouldn't be the same without Jackie!

He initially told me my habit of thanking him on various occasions felt unnatural, at least between Chinese couples. But I now catch him saying "thank you" to me as well. It is Jackie's presence here in China that gives me a warm feeling, a sense of home and hearth. Jackie taped a photo of himself with Jackie

HUTONG HEARTTHROBS

Chan to our front door to really mark the house as his abode, and when our Italian neighbor Marco saw it, he jokingly referred to our house as "The Jackie Chan House." Jackie's twin sister, when visiting us in the hutong house, astutely remarked that our home was very "warm" (the word she used was "温馨," which denotes both warmth and comfort).

It is up to Jackie and me to make the most of life and enjoy it. Now there is a sack of flour in the kitchen, and Jackie is wearing an apron with a bear on it, making dumplings. He freezes the dumplings for me to eat when he goes out on extended acting stints. "What a kind-hearted man," a friend remarked when I told her about Jackie's dumpling-making.

Once due to a maintenance emergency at our hutong house, I was unable to eat a warm meal before going to work because Jackie and I had to interact with the landlord to solve the issue, so on my way to the Yonghegong subway station, Jackie sprinted after me carrying a plastic container with his homemade dumplings which I could eat at the desk in our newsroom.

My bread-and-butter job is working at a state-run news agency in the heart of Beijing, either afternoons or nights, editing English-language news stories for global readers. We cover everything from formal bilateral ties stories and headlines material to a lot less earth-shattering news, e.g., the exchange rate of the Turkish lira, cattle counts and erosion in Mongolia, Tanzania issuing an alert over a red-eye disease outbreak, Nobel Prize winners as announced in Stockholm, a hot air balloon tragedy in Georgia that led to the electrocution of the three passengers after a collision with a power line, or a bus accident in Japan in which the passengers had a brush with death but ultimately only two people scraped their knees.... After work, I am happy to retreat from these real-world problems to the relatively blissful parallel universe of our hutong house.

In fact, Jackie is in charge of the cooking while I do other household tasks such as cleaning and some gardening, with Jackie occasionally watering or over-watering the plants, so there is a fair division of labor.

To spice up our cuisine, I have planted some tiny chili peppers in containers in our little courtyard especially for Jackie, as he enjoys plucking them when they are ripe and then popping them into his mouth at various meals. However, when I offered to do the cooking on some occasions when he was exhausted from his acting, his eyes widened apprehensively, and he asked, "Eat what?" In other words, someone with my questionable culinary skills had best stay out of the kitchen until it was time to do the dishes.

"Who does the cooking in your household?" a young Chinese once asked me. "My boyfriend," I replied, upon which he said, "You are very lucky." But it is my impression that having a girlfriend or wife who is a bad cook is still widely considered a real bummer in China.

Next to cooking, Jackie can also darn clothes and sew on buttons very well using firm and efficient stitches. When I was growing up, our beloved nanny tried unsuccessfully to teach me how to sew well; she minced no words and said, "You darn like the devil."

"Where did you learn sewing?" I asked Jackie, slightly surprised.

"Oh, definitely in the army!" he replied.

When I am out, Jackie occasionally sends me messages to check in. I know it is Jackie when I hear multiple "beeps" because unlike my other WeChat friends, Jackie sends me a volley of messages and stickers at a time instead of just one or two. Jackie and I get along splendidly, and although there are small misunderstandings—we speak Chinese, and I am still working on becoming more proficient — it is going pretty smoothly on the whole.

I was born in the Year of the Snake, and Jackie in the Year of the Rooster, and the signs are considered to be very compatible; the Snake is the "little Dragon" in the Chinese zodiac, because the Snake follows the formidable Dragon zodiac sign and some of the power and good luck are said to rub off on the Snake from the Dragon, whereas the Rooster is considered to be like a "phoenix." The Dragon (male) and Phoenix (female) iconography stand for the complementarity of a married couple (in Chinese history, emperor and empress, respectively). When Jackie was biking in the Qinling Mountains in his native Shaanxi province once after I had returned to the US in 2012, he encountered a small snake on a mountain road. "This is Tammy," he thought to himself and using a stick, gently picked up and placed the snake on the roadside so it wouldn't get injured by motorists.

Indeed, Jackie and I hardly ever fight, and even when we do, I know I will always lose because Chinese isn't my mother tongue. Still, Jackie said he believes we speak a "common language," despite the fact that we have two mother tongues. What's more, Jackie and I can sense when the other is tense or when something is amiss and we can often anticipate each other's needs.

Differences in lifestyle are not much of an issue, and the only thing that drives me crazy is Jackie's extensive dress shoe and sneaker collection as well as the colorful socks, flashy jewelry and bling Jackie leaves lying around the house (a cross-shaped pendant usually worn by rappers is the latest addition to his accessories). After all, he is an actor and born in the Year of the Rooster (with Roosters allegedly wanting to dress up and preen).

Jackie tends to misplace various items such as his house key or subway card. I told him he may place his key and subway card anywhere at his discretion, but I have ensured Jackie's important documents are stored in a safe place.

However, I like Jackie's whimsical additions to the household, for example a fuzzy toilet seat cover with teddy bears on it, which reads "Happy Bear," or a shower cap that features a big smiley face and the slogan "Always smile." And his quirks—he has a habit of rearranging things in a humorous way, for instance, he put an empty liquor bottle in the refrigerator and stuck a chocolate rose bud in it that had been part of a birthday cake. And I once caught him running around with a toothbrush sticking out of the pocket on the back of his shorts.

Meanwhile, Jackie, who is not only photogenic but has an eye for taking photos, is incredibly picky when it comes to my taking photos or videos of him. "Where are my legs?" he asked several times when I had accidentally left them out because I was in a hurry. So I fuss with the camera until I get shots and video clips that satisfy him. "Remember, there are two Liu Pengs (Jackies). The one who is on set and the one who is off set," he reminded me on one of those occasions. In fact, actors like Jackie often have multiple personae; and it was up to me to accept and love them all.

The same applies when Jackie is on the other end of the camera. When it comes to any kind of camera work, Jackie is extremely critical and has high standards, whereas I am a lot more relaxed. For example, when he helped me make an audition video on his smart phone for a movie role featuring former US President Harry Truman's "frumpy but efficient" secretary, Rose Conway, a historical figure (I occasionally engage in acting stints in Beijing and this was a role I was lusting after but ultimately didn't get), Jackie immediately rejected the first audition video we made.

"Look how you are holding the folder," he said, referring to a report I was supposed to carry to President Truman, played by Jackie. "It doesn't look good. We have to do another take." And he came over, gently adjusted the way I was holding what was supposed to look like a folder (actually a big old manila envelope with material for this book) and reshot the video, with the small hutong house courtyard serving as the White House Oval Office.

Domestic harmony is the norm. When we travel, we are both heavy packers, so you can imagine our caravan of luggage, which makes me dread the prospect of moving house. What's more, Jackie likes to save a lot of odds and ends to reuse and this is a commendable trait; however, things start to pile up quickly in a small hutong house. And I occasionally have an urge to act like a packrat and store things of sentimental value.

For instance, Jackie recently called me over. "Look at this!" he said, cradling a tiny black box in the palm of his hand. "This is the phone I used to call you the first time!" I looked at this relic of a bygone era. How simple and unsophisticated this mobile phone seemed compared to today's smart phones! We decided to keep it as this small, unpretentious item had enabled our relationship over long, long distances. If it weren't for that simple mobile phone, there would be no relationship between us today.

However, he can get touchy when I try to clean up his corners, although I try to be minimally invasive and leave everything more or less in its original place for him. I call Jackie's messes his nests and yes, a man's messes can drive women absolutely insane.

Indeed, as my Singaporean friend Beixi once wrote me in an email, "Love is not only about passion and romance, but also about 'taking out the trash'"—meaning overcoming the irritations and hardships of life together. Jackie, like most Chinese, did not have the habit of going to the dentist for a check-up and cleaning every year, although this might be changing as Chinese now have more disposable income, and are taking better care of themselves. But many Americans religiously go to the dentist on an annual or even semi-annual basis, including me.

So one year, I suggested Jackie come with me and we both get our check-ups and cleanings together, even though he has wonderfully straight and healthy teeth. While our dentist pokes around in my mouth and pricks my gums, Jackie holds my hand, and when it is time for him to climb into the dentist's chair, I soothe his nerves. I am hoping Jackie and I can still have all our original teeth, more or less, when we are eighty years old.

For my part, I did additional hand-holding when Jackie had a fish bone stuck in this throat and had to have it removed in a hospital. Although many Chinese are adept at the art of picking the bones from a fish while eating it, Jackie wasn't careful that time. I waited outside the consulting room, twiddling my thumbs and garnering a lot of stares as the only foreigner there. It was a military hospital in Beijing and I was impressed by their no-frills, efficient approach. A no-nonsense nurse pushed me out of the room, not allowing me to watch the actual procedure and distract as they pulled the fine bone out through Jackie's nose with a hook.

After only ten minutes, Jackie triumphantly emerged, showing everyone waiting outside the fish bone after it had been successfully dislodged from his throat. He even showed the fine, tiny bone to others while we were taking the elevator down before I urged him to either immediately pocket the bone or dispose of it. I was greatly relieved and even a bit amused after spending a rather nerve-racking two days due to Jackie's fish bone ordeal, with his mother calling in and giving me instructions that if drinking vinegar didn't help to break down the stubborn little bone, to take her son to the hospital.

Yet another difference is that Jackie likes to wash his clothes by hand, as he did when he was a soldier. He cannot get used to the washing machine, whereas I cannot do without it. But we always hang out our clothes to dry together; after all, most households in China don't have dryers. Verily, "the best kind of harmony is household harmony," as my father used to say.

And occasionally, I need my Western food fix, like pepperoni pizza for breakfast whereas Jackie relishes a traditional Chinese breakfast of porridge, which he slurps down (in China, slurping soup or porridge conveys appreciation of the food, not bad manners), bread and hard-boiled eggs. Speaking of eggs, Jackie purchases eggs from free-range chickens in bulk via Douyin (the Chinese TikTok) from a man in Chongqing who proudly proclaimed, "My chickens are my superstars."

"Free-range chickens are happier so they lay better-quality eggs," Jackie, a fervent animal lover, believes.

For lunch or dinner, I occasionally enjoy a grilled hamburger, but when a Chinese friend asked Jackie whether he also relishes that American staple, Jackie diplomatically replied, "I grew up in the countryside, so I'm not picky when it comes to food." To enhance the atmosphere of our dinners, I like to light candles, either tea candles or taper candles. When Jackie once posted a photo of our candlelit dinner on social media, a Chinese netizen was puzzled: "Why did you light candles?" he asked. In my experience, many Chinese use candles only on temple visits or for birthday cakes, but not to create a cozy or romantic atmosphere. But Jackie immediately understood and appreciated what I was aiming for when I put a candle on our dinner table—namely a romantic dinner for two—and quickly followed suit when we were running out of candlesticks by buying more.

Also, when Jackie has a fever, I apply a washcloth soaked in warm water to his forehead and give him a cup of warm water to drink, Chinese style, whereas I prefer to cool off with a washcloth soaked in cold water, American style, when I am running a fever and pop an ibuprofen. I wonder how many cups of warm or hot water I have prepared for Jackie since we met as a small love service.

On occasion, Jackie likes to have some coffee for breakfast, although it made him feel giddy at the beginning. He even learned how to grill hamburgers, a skill he showed off to a Chinese friend. He once bought a bottle of salad dressing without being sure what it was; he merely thought it looked interesting. The bottle of salad dressing was in our refrigerator for several days. One day, for lunch, Jackie made a mixed salad, among other dishes, and I remembered the dressing and put the bottle on the table. "How do you use this?" Jackie asked. After overcoming my surprise, I told him to just pour the contents over the salad. I also taught Jackie how to hold a wine glass, and how Americans use tape — we bend strips of tape into curls and tack them onto the back of paper.

Meanwhile, Jackie was "Sinicizing" me by inspiring in me a love for dumplings and showing me how to bite into garlic cloves (Chinese social media users got a kick out of seeing me peeling and eating huge garlic cloves in a small video). I also got used to drinking hot or warm water instead of cold, but my beer needs to be served cold, no piss warm beer for me, please. However, Jackie and I never attempt to change who the other is at the core. And every day with Jackie brings new discoveries and experiences!

I feel very blessed to have Jackie at my side. "It takes one hundred years for a couple to meet (take the same boat) and one thousand years to share a pillow," he once told me, reciting a famous Chinese saying ("百年修得同船渡，千年修得共枕眠"). If your counterpart comes from a different culture, that not only adds to the challenges, but also to the rewards.

Although Western women dating Asian men may still seem somewhat "niche," I am sure it is a growing trend because interracial relationships on the whole are becoming more common. To cater to this growing trend, there is a WeChat group dedicated to Western women with Chinese (Asian) men in Beijing called Beijing WWAM, which stands for Western Women and Asian Men.

The Beijing WWAM group, which has several spin-offs in other cities, now has more than 160 members; when I joined, it had about 130 members. The members discuss the challenges of being in a relationship with a Chinese man. For example, what documents are needed to get married to a Chinese citizen in China, or finding day care for children with foreign passports. Some foreign women complain their Chinese husbands are like "spoiled children" and don't help with household tasks and rearing children, so they use the WeChat group to vent or ask for advice on how to better communicate with their partners and spouses. Others, however, say they are very satisfied with their Chinese men and believe they do a good job at helping out at home.

Some problems are definitely culture-specific, and I greatly enjoy the group comments. For example, one foreign woman living with her Chinese partner had to cover up the vanity table mirror in her bedroom because her partner's grandmother, who was living right below them, believed it brought bad luck to have a mirror facing the bed.

Another foreign woman living in the same building as her in-laws but in a separate apartment sometimes got unexpected visits from her in-laws and the granny, who had keys to her and her Chinese husband's apartment because the relatives were the owners. This made her quite uncomfortable as she liked to lounge about the apartment in her underwear. Different ideas about what constitutes privacy in East and West can spark conflict, and WWAM members gave fascinating input on this. In a nutshell, respect, communication, compassion and occasional compromise are the keys to solving numerous cross-cultural conflicts, but of course, this is easier said than done.

While some couples are battling it out about the division of household labor or other domestic issues, Jackie and I rarely have such disagreements; Jackie protested once when I used a commanding tone asking him to buy more beer—usually he jokes that I am "the boss," but this time he was visibly annoyed—and I quickly apologized. Erich Segal's catchphrase for his novel *Love Story* was "Love means never having to say you're sorry." Ali MacGraw, who played Jenny in the movie adaptation of the novel, rightfully commented that that is a complete crock. Love does sometimes mean having to say you're sorry.

The situation of migrant workers in our neighborhood is often worrying. They come to Beijing for more opportunities and a better life (they have counterparts in other major Chinese cities such as Shanghai and Guangzhou). There are some in our neighborhood; some work as delivery workers. One woman worked as a dish washer in the neighborhood and she may also have held other jobs. Her son, who was in grade school, was struggling with his English so I agreed to help him with his homework on one occasion.

But migrant workers, a segment of the population that contributes greatly to Beijing's vitality and growth, do not have Beijing residence rights and therefore cannot access basic social services, such as public schooling or subsidized medical care, and cannot buy property in Beijing. Moreover, if a migrant worker wants to get married, or apply for a new Chinese identity card or a passport, they must return to their hometown. This household registration system, known as the *hukou* system, is in place to contain the flow of the population to larger cities.

I knew a young Chinese man of humble origins in China's

South who had been accepted by one of China's top universities, and upon graduation was able to secure a job in Beijing that offered him a Beijing residence permit. He later found a respectable job at a Fortune 500 company. This kind of man is known in China as a "phoenix man" (*fenghuangnan* or 凤凰男) — a man who had grown up in China's rural areas, attended university, and secured a good job in the city. The term may have originated from a saying, "山窝里飞出的金凤凰," which loosely translates as "a golden phoenix soars out of a chicken coop."

However, this "phoenix man" was considered undateable and unmarriageable in Beijing because he was struggling to afford an apartment, a prerequisite for marriage and he thus experienced a perennial sense of crisis. He told me he had been getting along very well with a prospective girlfriend online, but when she asked whether he had an apartment and he said "no," she abruptly told him, "Then we have nothing more to say to each other."

"It's all about survival," the young man told me. "As a foreigner, you will never understand what it's like." He was right; as a foreigner who had grown up in a completely different place and under completely different circumstances, I could always peep into the windows of Chinese life, but I would never be on the other side of the wall.

A pragmatic approach to love and marriage is quite common in China; for example, my Chinese ex-boyfriend had told me with a straight face after seven years together, "Love is one thing, marriage another." I agree that loving someone may not be enough to make a marriage, but to me and many people around the world today, love should be the foundation.

But back to our hutong house neighborhood; the advantage of living in the hutongs is experiencing a lot of local flavor. One encounter with our neighbors was with a Chinese woman called Pan Xue (潘雪), who is known to foreign tourists by her English name, Joyce. She ran a dumpling-making workshop for foreigners in a hutong house she was renting several doors from us. She once sought my help in writing "vegetarian dishes" in attractive-looking English calligraphy on a blackboard outside her shop, and I was happy to assist. Afterwards, she invited Jackie and me over for some parties. On numerous occasions when I passed her workshop, it was full of foreigners donning aprons and merrily bearing down on rolling pins, engaging in a Beijing dumpling making-experience and photo-ops.

There was also an elderly Chinese man in the neighborhood whose English wasn't bad. When I first encountered him, he wore a military jacket that had "U.S.A." emblazoned on it, strangely paired with a small badge that said "Red Army." He liked to talk to foreigners, greeting them in English or smatterings of other foreign languages.

"Foreigners prize logic," he told Jackie and me in Chinese. "One is one in the West and two is two. Westerners say one word and it has one meaning, whereas one word can have multiple meanings if spoken by a Chinese," he said. He mostly came on too strong and his utterances sometimes resembled those of a Shakespearean fool, making some of our neighbors a bit uncomfortable. However, he did make some valuable observations and encouraged Jackie and me to learn more about each other's culture. Later, he was discovered by a Douyin (Tiktok) influencer and he became somewhat of a Douyin sensation after being interviewed and not just another neighborhood legend, and he seemed to revel in his newfound fame.

Next to the interactions with our neighbors, hutong house challenges keep Jackie and me on our toes. I have already mentioned some of the Spartan aspects of living in an old hutong house. One day, the electricity suddenly went out in the living room. We had run out of electricity and needed to buy more. I grew impatient, but then Jackie uttered what would to me become a classic line, "I thought you said you liked challenges!" Despite my annoyance, I had to slap my knee and laugh. He was right; on one occasion, I had admitted liking to be challenged.

One winter, our neighborhood suffered a blackout as the grid was overburdened; everyone, it appeared, was running their little electric heaters simultaneously. Again, I grew impatient and while Jackie was on the phone with our electricity provider, I stormed and let out an expletive I had probably learned from a Chinese TV series (it definitely wasn't from Jackie): "狗屁!" This word literally means "dog fart" but translates into "bullshit" or "crap" in English.

"Tammy!" Jackie exclaimed, shocked. "As someone with a PhD, you need to watch your reputation. You know, they might be recording our phone conversation!" Like a naughty child, I retreated into the bedroom.

After a few other incidents, I found myself asking Jackie, "Why are the Chinese so complicated?"

"Well, because of their five-thousand year history," Jackie replied, matter-of-factly. (Actually, China has more than three thousand years of written history; the five thousand years are proverbial.) That made sense, sort of. "You have chosen the complicated," he told me about my choice to live in China, and I would like to think that living here eventually makes one smarter and one's mind more nimble by sheer necessity. An African friend who was raising his twin teenage boys in Beijing and giving them an education in Chinese schools also commented while we were swapping expat stories over coffee, "You need to be tough to live here" and "China makes us (foreigners) stronger."

My advice for living here is don't sweat the small stuff; conserve your energy and pace yourself. And fasten your seatbelts; try to enjoy the ride despite the occasional turbulence.

———∞∞———

One of the reasons I so enjoy being with Jackie is because he is a sunny and optimistic person and always sees the silver lining in the cloud.

When we were hunkering down during the Spring Festival in 2020 and for days on end afterward as a preventive measure due to the spread of Covid-19, Jackie said, smiling, "Now we have an opportunity to be together every day!"

After many days spent almost exclusively inside, watching movies or scrolling through Douyin, sleeping and eating, Jackie realized the stamina it takes not only to remain inside for days on end, facing an uncertain and somewhat frightening situation, but also being cut off from most of the world. Jackie was far away from his family in Shaanxi, and I was even farther, of course, from my family back in the US and Germany, with an ever smaller window of opportunity to leave the country as the virus spread. It was frightening.

I had chosen to tough it out with Jackie because I was confident in our relationship, confident in our love, and confident that China would eventually conquer the virus with some help from the international community. "Baobei (宝贝 means "darling" or "baby"), thank you for sticking things out with me, I am very moved," Jackie told me one morning, with tears in his eyes.

I would never consider leaving Jackie behind! At the beginning of the Covid-19 outbreak in China, my gut instinct was to take Jackie with me to the US to flee the virus as my mother had suggested but this did not prove to be a viable solution for numerous reasons. Then, the tables turned as China brought the virus under control for a while, with Jackie and me sitting in Beijing, watching in horror as the virus spread rapidly through the US and the rest of the world. It felt like being in a Stephen King novel with the endless unpleasant surprises.

But the months after China decided to join the rest of the world in living with the virus starting in December 2022 and just let it rip found me lapsing into depression, the nadir being my sitting in the bathroom on our "porcelain throne," drinking whisky out of a crystal cocktail glass and sobbing in the wee hours of the morning. There were just too many changes, and they were coming too quickly.

Jackie was challenged with getting me back on my feet. Once measures were somewhat relaxed, he proposed going to the movies, visiting museums, and cycling around Beijing to get my mind on more positive things; and it helped to a large extent. Indeed, the virus became a litmus test of established order and of many relationships around the world.

———∞———

Jackie gives me advice about dealing with Chinese people, which facilitates my social interactions with them. This means adopting some characteristics and mannerisms that would please the Chinese without effacing who I truly am as a Westerner. Some things, like not being loud or proud, are never really much of a problem for me as I strike most people as a rather quiet, low-key person. Other things would prove to be more difficult, for example, getting used to a communication style that can be ambiguous and indirect, and being flexible!

"Remember, be polite when the landlord comes as contracts don't exist in Chinese people's minds," Jackie said. In other words, I needed to be flexible when navigating Chinese society.

Jackie later drew a diagram for me showing two dots, or two Westerners, with arrows pointing straight at each other, showing their straightforward communication style. Then below it,

Jackie drew another diagram showing another two dots, or two Chinese people, with arrows going off in all directions from one dot, and making lasso-like loops, before reaching the opposite dot, showing their roundabout communication style.

"Chinese first consider who you are, what your background is, and the situation before replying to you," Jackie said. That, of course, does not mean Westerners don't do the same thing, just not nearly as much. Reasons for the "round" way of thinking include not wanting to offend someone, to show respect for those in authority and not to invite retribution by causing resentment.

Sometimes foreigners are expected to mask emotions when interacting with Chinese. "I'm tired of always having to smile and be nice!" a clearly frustrated young Ukrainian woman in Beijing once told me. Personally, I occasionally found it hard and annoying as well to keep my true thoughts and feelings under wraps except at home or with people I truly trusted; in other words, muzzling myself. Coming from the US, where people tend to say exactly what is on their minds, it was a difficult transition. But approaching life in China as an ongoing acting job made it easier for me.

Some Chinese, Jackie included, also occasionally tire of having to mask their thoughts and emotions. Jackie once told me he enjoys talking to me "because I don't have to think half a day about what to say," as our communication is simple and straightforward. I do wonder, therefore, about communication between Chinese couples.

Due to the ongoing limits of my Chinese, Jackie and I don't engage in any in-depth political discussions, although some superficial conversation might be possible. We don't miss anything as a result because we simply aren't very political people, even though I grew up in the capital of the United States, Washington, D.C., with my armchair politician father.

HUTONG HEARTTHROBS

But Jackie was shocked by Douyin posts that detailed violence against people of Asian descent in the US during the Covid-19 pandemic. The posts helped to convince him that America isn't the utopia depicted in some Hollywood films.

"Better stay in China!" he concluded. I gave Jackie a hug and reassured him that we would definitely go to visit the US one day so he could see where I had grown up, and most importantly, finally meet my mother (to date, Jackie and my mother had only interacted via Zoom as I translated). I vowed to myself that I would ensure he would have a safe and pleasant experience.

Another thing that I found challenging next to their indirect way of expressing themselves was the flexibility of many Chinese. One example concerned our communal trash bins, which featured fancy pulley mechanisms so that we didn't have to touch the handles on the lids to open them. They were located right next to the red wall of the Imperial Academy/Confucius Temple complex. Everything had gone very well in the past, with everyone disposing of their trash and organic waste in the designated bins more or less in an orderly manner. I felt very proud of living in such a progressively orderly and civilized neighborhood.

But one night, our two trash bins and those of our neighbors disappeared, much to my consternation. I suspected we would have to wait for the trash pedicabs to arrive as they do twice daily, and hand over our garbage bags directly. This would be incredibly inconvenient. I hadn't come to China to wait around for garbage trucks!

I hid behind one house wall the next evening to watch how an elderly neighbor disposed of his trash—a tiny trash bag and an old backpack. He looked around furtively and hesitated before placing the items against the wall, where the trash bins used to be. Maybe Jackie and I should follow his lead.

"Hi, Tammy, what are you doing here?" I spun around. It was Marco, our Italian neighbor, on his bicycle.

"I'm just watching how our neighbor is disposing of his trash," I whispered.

"I know, they removed the trash bins, hopefully just to clean them," Marco replied. "It's too soon for me to get worried. Let me know if you hear any updates."

Perhaps Marco was more carefree as an Italian, or perhaps he was in denial, I thought; if it was the first, I really envied him. Yet it wasn't too early for me, as a half-German, to worry.

Other trash bags were unceremoniously dumped next to the Imperial Academy wall, with a neighborhood dog gleefully rummaging through them for food as if it were a buffet while his owner sitting in a motorized wheelchair looked on approvingly. Meanwhile, we residents were told to wait for the whistle that announces the passage of the tiny garbage truck. I thought the notion of having us listen for a whistle like dogs was highly distasteful. But when I told Jackie about our newest garbage disposal woes, he remained cool and collected and wasn't concerned at all, simply suggesting we dispose of the trash in the public trash bins on the main street next to our hutongs. And that's what we did. "Be a bit flexible," Jackie urged me. I scowled.

Bruce Lee, who was not only a formidable kung fu master but also a philosopher bridging East and West, advised that it is best to "be like water" and "bend" to survive. In other words, be flexible. But still, even after ten years in China, I occasionally think to myself: Damn it! I may score tiny, temporary victories now and then, but I am constantly in a state of checkmate here by forces greater than myself. The only things that kept me playing—besides my love for Jackie—were my stubborn nature and curiosity to see what lay ahead. It is my experience that those old China hands who fare the best in China just enjoy the game and don't fret too much about the outcome. They don't play to win.

I make one big exception to the first "Be flexible" commandment for living in China, and that concerns people who cut in front of others standing in line. Jumping the queue seems to be a favorite pastime for some people in China. However, I am sensing some change in this, perhaps due to an increasing awareness that this isn't considered polite by universal standards. For my part, I don't think it is wrong to politely remind people to wait their turn in queues, no matter where I am.

As a half-American, half-German, I dare say I have become a bit more flexible over the years. Instead of always meticulously planning ahead, I now find myself going more with the flow, improvising more, enjoying more, and thus feeling more relaxed by using a "wait and see approach."

This was further borne out in 2021 shortly before the American Thanksgiving Day when I was spending more time at home due to the Covid outbreak and engaging in "home office." I was busy redecorating our hutong house with Jackie's input. I surprised myself by suspending strings of pink heart-shaped beads around the bedroom ceiling lamp in a kind of disorderly semi-circle instead of in an orderly full circle as a kind of homemade "chandelier."

I was strangely delighted by my new aesthetic appreciation for the slightly chaotic and random. Previously, it would have bothered me greatly if a circle wasn't neat and symmetrical. How strange, I thought. Tammy, what has happened to you? "The shape of the circle looks like your haircut," Jackie said with a grin, referring to my bob.

TAMMY TREICHEL

"So many hearts," Jackie mused, lying flat on the bed and staring up at the chandelier on the ceiling. "How many hearts are there?" I did the math: thirty strings of beads with five hearts on each string. One hundred and fifty hearts.

"I feel as if we are living in a hotel!" Jackie exclaimed. I giggled; hotels are widely associated with one-night stands. That special chandelier would come to witness us on many occasions cuddled up together underneath the feather covers, until the rosy-fingered dawn would peep through the hutong house curtains to rouse us.

I reasoned that it was either China that had changed me or getting older was making me mellower, more accepting of imperfections and flaws and finding unexpected beauty in them. It might also have been a survival mechanism as being a perfectionist is very energy-consuming and not necessarily healthy.

As with humor, sometimes there are differences in aesthetics, such as taste in furniture, decor, clothing, and so on. Jackie is in the habit of hanging his clothes to dry from clothes hangers all over the hutong house. It originally annoyed me because it looked slummy, but now I just close one eye and accept it as part of his "artistic mess." Coming to China as a foreigner is like experiencing a heart transplant—either your body accepts or rejects the new organ. My Chinese heart was working quite all right, beating more or less strongly each day.

How important respect for authority and face are in Chinese society has been borne out by some of my interactions with Jackie. For example, on one occasion, the police posted a "warm reminder" in the form of stickers on the walls of our neighborhood to lock our doors and windows and prevent fires. Jackie said we should leave the sticker in its original place on our hutong house wall to "give the police face." Moreover, Jackie genuinely believed the sticker was ideally placed next to our front door to discourage potential thieves.

But I wasn't very concerned about being robbed, given there were security cameras everywhere and our windows facing the street are covered by prison-like iron bars. I was more concerned about the unsightliness of the sticker; after all, its message conveyed just another piece of common sense to me. Yet I left it in its place, heeding Jackie's advice.

Jackie's attachment to the great value of "face," which he shares with most Chinese, was highlighted on a trip we took to Changsha, in Hunan province. After several long hours on the high-speed train, we arrived at our guesthouse. Hunan is known for its spicy food, passionate people, and the never-ending clacking of mahjong tiles. It is also the place where I discovered the joy of chewing betel nuts. The proprietress of the inn, something of a "hot Hunan girl" herself, greeted us hospitably—a bit too hospitably for my taste as I was tired and just wanted to check into our room as Jackie and I had a rigorous day of touring ahead. It seemed to me she was flirting with Jackie, who still appeared very jolly despite the long trip but oblivious to her advances.

As a side note, I was once asked by a friend whether I felt jealous when Jackie was on film sets surrounded by beautiful ladies. The answer is: Not really, because we trust each other. Plus, I reasoned, Jackie told me he likes foreign ladies who are "cultured," and it would be hard to find another American PhD girlfriend on a film set in China.

As I was trying to sort out the rather confusing details at the reception desk regarding payment and local taxes, I spotted a spider as large as the palm of my hand crawling up the wall behind the proprietress.

"Oh, look, a spider!" I exclaimed, my voice trembling slightly at the sight of what resembled a tarantula.

"It eats mosquitoes," the proprietress replied, nonchalantly, then turned back to Jackie to chat. As we climbed the stairs to our room, Jackie whispered, "I had hoped you wouldn't mention the spider to her as it wouldn't give her face!"

In our household, I largely deal with the finances, whereas Jackie is the "communicator" with China at large. Jackie once confessed to me, "I don't like money. Maybe I have never had the happiness of having a lot of it."

"Money can be your friend, don't be afraid of it," I replied. "You need to know how to make it work for you." I hope I wasn't sounding too much like an ultra-capitalist there. Still, Jackie has never felt comfortable dealing with financial matters, so I deal with them. Actually, I enjoy it and have become more financially capable as a result. As long as one partner in a couple deals well with the finances, I think it works.

I admit that in most situations, however, Jackie tends to see the bigger picture. Jackie and I often approach problems differently and come up with different solutions to them. Here is an example.

I am in the habit of taking a certain night bus home from work if I am on the night shift at the news agency I work at. The London-style double-decker bus played tunes such as the romantic "Jasmine Flower" or jazz, and we passed the beautifully lit Tian'anmen Square on our way to Yonghegong, so taking the bus was usually a joy ride.

As I was taking the bus home after my shift one winter night with Jackie, who was in the habit of escorting me home from work if he had time, an elderly woman got angry because she had missed her stop. So she held the driver, security guard and two passengers (Jackie and me) "hostage," grounding the "ghost bus," as a coworker referred to the night bus, on the highway and hurling obscenities.

HUTONG HEARTTHROBS

While talking to the complaint hotline, the elderly woman mentioned there were also "two (*sic*) foreigners" on the bus (meaning me and Jackie, whom she mistook for a foreigner because he was wrapped in a coat and wearing a large beaver hat). I don't know how the fact that there was a foreign presence on the bus would support her case, but I suppose she had left reason at the wayside in the heat of the moment.

The driver, a woman, was very professional and reacted little, and when she did, it was polite and restrained. The security guard just seemed annoyed and clearly wanting a break from the drama, stepped out of the bus, which was parked on the curb of the highway, dark and getting colder by the minute at minus three degrees Celsius outside. Jackie and I followed suit for a breath of fresh air. After the elderly woman had stepped out herself to take photos of the bus's license plate in the back, the guard, Jackie and myself climbed quickly back into the bus; we were acting out of instinct and just wanted to get away from the troublemaker.

A rather wicked thought crossed my mind. "Good," I thought to myself, "the driver will now step on the gas and we will resume our trip, leaving the old woman in the dust!" I was truly irritated at the delay and the increasing cold. But alas, the elderly woman also shuffled in rather quickly and continued with her verbal abuse, which even included cussing the driver's family, taking photos of the driver with her smart phone and even pointing it at the rest of us like a magic wand. Luckily, it was dark and we were well disguised in our winter clothing, so I trust no one could be identified on her photos. I remember hoping she wouldn't post the photos on social media and cause embarrassment. In today's world, that's akin to being forced to walk the plank.

In between the woman's foul-mouthed tirade, I managed to crawl up to the front and ask the driver what we should do as, of course, Jackie and I needed to continue our journey. Meanwhile, Jackie was paralyzed in his seat. Like many Chinese, he was afraid of being involved in any way because of fear of reprisal or legal implications, and of course of having photos of us landing on the elderly woman's WeChat, Douyin or Kuaishou (a video-sharing platform akin to Douyin) account.

For my part, I was more worried about immediate threats: being stranded in the dark, freezing and catching cold. The driver said we should wait inside for the next bus on that route to come, which we did. When it arrived within ten minutes, the driver helped Jackie and me board the new bus before returning to her "mother ship" and the elderly woman.

This incident caused a delay of maybe half an hour for Jackie and me. After all, we were traveling on a highway, and although the place we were taken "hostage" at wasn't far from our home, it was still a long distance to walk and hard to get a taxi on the highway, should we have chosen to "jump ship."

When I told Jackie later I had hoped the driver would just step on the gas and drive away with us, while the elderly woman was taking photos of the license plate outside, Jackie said, "*Baobei*, it was a public bus!" In other words, the driver was bound to protocol and couldn't just strand a passenger, no matter how disruptive he or she was behaving. Also, Jackie reminded me that the elderly woman had probably been slow with her reflexes and thus maybe unable to react in a timely manner when her stop came, which might have explained her frustration. This showed that Jackie tends to see the bigger picture as opposed to me, at least when I am blinded by feelings. "True," I replied, "but that elderly woman sure had a quick reflex when it came to opening her mouth and hurling obscenities!"

In China, the elderly are traditionally always considered "right," no matter how they behave. A Chinese coworker told me she thought elderly people should be respected because of their age, no matter what their transgressions. In principle, I also think elderly people should naturally be respected and helped, but not if they misbehave, disrupt public order or are downright mean.

To me, the elderly woman's tirade was off-putting, and I think she may have come to a quicker and more efficient solution to her problem if she had asked the driver for assistance instead of verbally attacking her. In any case, Jackie said that if he were the bus driver, he would have given the old woman 100 yuan (about USD 14) out of his own pocket to take a cab home. That was a generous approach to things and something I never would have considered.

On a practical level, Jackie has also taught me some kitchen "hacks" or tricks, and shared a recipe for a winter drink with me. It tastes like punch, and Jackie said he likes it because it is warm, fills you up, is nutritious, and doesn't make you too tipsy. I call the drink "Jackie's holiday punch" and it is a good beverage for either Christmas or the Spring Festival. It is great to soothe your nerves after your bus is hijacked, for example.

JACKIE'S PUNCH

Ingredients:
- One bottle of beer (Jackie and I prefer Beijing Yanjing beer, 燕京啤酒)
- A 400g jar or container of rice wine (米酒)
- A handful of wolfberries (枸杞)

Directions:
Heat up the beer, let it simmer, not boil. Add the rice wine and wolfberries. Let the flavors mingle for several minutes and then

pour into mugs. Serves 1-2 people.

On a deeper level, Jackie said that in China, you need connections (关系, *guanxi*) and ability (能力, *nengli*) to survive, whereas in the West, ability is paramount. Connections are, of course, important anywhere, but in my experience they are somewhat more important in China, where you often count on your contacts to open doors, get you out of trouble, or simply make life easier.

Jackie also gave me some advice on how to interact with Chinese people. When I favorably mentioned the Deng Lijun (aka Teresa Teng) restaurant in Beijing on my WeChat, a coworker commented that her mother might like the venue and asked how to get there. "Take your mother to Babaoshan (八宝山)," I was about to reply in Chinese, simply and to the point. Babaoshan is a subway stop close to a famous cemetery in Beijing, from which it derives its name.

"Stop!" Jackie cried, using the actual English word before I hit the reply button. "You are asking your coworker to take her mother to *Babaoshan*?" He immediately helped me rewrite the reply, ensuring there was no double entendre. In China, anything death-related is still pretty much taboo and needs to be handled with extra care.

Similarly, when I was invited to be a judge in a children's talent show, Jackie would again provide me with valuable advice on how to navigate the cultural divide. The children were incredibly talented and well-behaved; they had a great stage presence and were completely unfazed by foreigners. My favorite performer was a small boy I nicknamed "Tiny Tim" because he was the smallest of the group, rapping in an oversized sweater and sneakers. It was another feel-good experience in China.

Some of the children were asked to write essays based on an informal interview with me. When I was asked by one girl about the most important quality a news reporter should have, I answered in Chinese, "connections" (搞关系 or *gao guanxi* means "making contacts/networking")—and I could tell by her confused expression and her mother's displeasure that it had been the wrong answer—in that given social and cultural context.

After my gaffe, Jackie discreetly took me aside and said that the correct Chinese answer in this setting was "study well" (好好学习, *hao hao xuexi*), the common aspiration of Chinese youngsters that is instilled into them by their parents from an early age. That was the answer I used for the next child and it was satisfactory. I should have considered my audience—I was talking to a child, not to an adult, and I also needed to give the Chinese host an answer they wanted to hear, as their guest.

Jackie also took issue with an article I later wrote about that experience, pointing to my sense of self-aggrandizement from a Chinese point of view, because I obviously enjoyed basking in the children's attention. After all, Chinese traditionally set great store by modesty, whereas Westerners like to exude self-confidence and draw attention to themselves. I vowed to keep my big ego more under control.

Going deeper, sometimes when I was stumped, I sought answers from China's most venerated sage, Confucius, whose temple here in Beijing was just several meters away from our hutong house. I visited Confucius' hometown of Qufu in Shandong province with Jackie in May 2017.

"Study the Confucian *Analects* (论语) if you want to understand China better," a close Chinese friend once advised me. So before moving to China, I bought a copy of British orientalist Arthur Waley's translation of the *Analects*, and I must say my friend's advice was among the best I have ever received. In China, you can run but you can't hide from Confucius.

The thrust of Confucius' philosophy is preserving social order and harmony; he was not concerned with the metaphysical. One of my Chinese teachers said Confucius appeals to many people because of his work ethic, emphasis on social order and deference to elders, whereas others tend to look to the philosopher Lao Tzu (also known as Lao Zi, 老子), the founder of Taoism (Daoism), for wisdom because of his emphasis on peacefulness and being one with nature.

Jackie had opened so many doors for me, and I tried to pry some doors open for him, too, for example by introducing him to my foreign friends so that he could broaden his horizons. After all, he had gone abroad only once so far for film work. Although Jackie can be shy when meeting my foreign friends, especially around those who don't speak Chinese, I always encourage him to jump into the fray.

For instance, I introduced Jackie to an Indian man called Shastri. Although Shastri didn't speak Chinese, we still had a wonderful meal at an Indian restaurant with me as a go-between and *ad hoc* translator. Shastri ate with his hands, I with a knife and fork and Jackie with chopsticks. On this occasion, Jackie found the concept of going Dutch somewhat alien. Had the host been Chinese, all expenses would likely have been covered; whoever invites, foots the bill.

Daniel K. Schweitzer is another friend of Jackie's and mine. He is a German photographer, and he asked if he could visit Jackie and me in our hutong house for a photo session. We agreed, and he produced a series of unusual images of Jackie and me posing in traditional Chinese garb in our neighborhood. Some of our neighbors were puzzled by the red yarn Daniel tied around Jackie and myself to demonstrate his abstract theme of "Oneness." In my favorite photo, he conveyed a sense of timelessness with elements from traditional China (costumes, the hutong houses) blending in with modern appliances (bicycles, air conditioners and solar panels).

These have been some of my thoughts on home life with Jackie, as I enter the late summer of my life. When the weather is warm, Jackie and I like to dine in the tiny courtyard of the hutong house and watch the cats jumping across the eaves or the leaves of the old poplar tree next to our home swaying in the wind.

7

CARPE DIEM IN CHINA

During our first autumn in the hutong house together, Jackie asked me one day what I thought of our old poplar tree whose leaves had all fallen down. Despite the extra work the tree caused us in terms of having to remove its leaves that were littering our courtyard, I said I liked it very much, especially with the sun setting behind it. After all, it has been Beijing's majestic poplars with their nodding silver heads that have greeted me every time I entered the city. Jackie said some of the trees in Beijing are hundreds of years old, and will see many more generations and happenings long after we are gone. So, seize the day!

And this is exactly what Jackie and I have been doing in Beijing.

I enjoy occasions such as the Mid-Autumn or Moon Festival, which is like the Chinese Thanksgiving, with family members sitting at a round table sharing a meal and watching the luminous, full mid-autumn moon. And, of course, Halloween. Indeed, Western holidays have taken on a new significance for me in China, as I see them in a new light and also share them with Chinese friends. The Chinese festivals touch a chord with me as they are often centered on family. These festivals bring me special joy as I can share them with Jackie and learn more about the Chinese festivals from him, whereas I teach him about the Western festivals. Another cultural exchange.

Jackie and I carved our first pumpkin for Halloween together, using chopsticks as a drill and a knife for carving, and strolled around the neighborhood on the evening. Nearby Wudaoying (五道营) hutong was especially spooky, the bars there were festooned with Halloween decorations and eerie music emanated from them. There was a woman selling headbands topped with axes, and modeled them on her dog. There were also several trick-or-treaters who solicited the establishments under the watchful eyes of their parents, although none ever came to knock on the door of our hutong house.

One year for Halloween, I dressed as a suffragette, a woman from the early 20th century fighting for the right to vote, with a historically accurate sash I had made out of paper, and Jackie was my supporter, in a pirate costume minus the hat. The following Halloween saw me as Little Orphan Annie in an orange clown wig and with freckles painted on my face, and Jackie as my sweet, handsome pirate companion again. And no, we didn't go trick-or-treating...

TAMMY TREICHEL

On Halloween 2015, in our Yonghegong neighborhood, many locals were burning paper money and paper clothes. Joining in the custom, Jackie and I on one occasion also burned paper money on the anniversary of my father's death. When I told my mother she said, "I doubt your father, a businessman, would have approved of that." I assured her that it was not real money, of course. Until it reaches the spirit world, that is.

There is a similar day in China dedicated to the dead called the Hungry Ghost Festival, at the end of summer, which has Daoist and Buddhist origins. On that day, Chinese people leave sacrifices of food to appease the ghosts of the deceased who roam the earth. So don't be alone and get home early.

As Halloween was again approaching one year, my mother asked me over the phone, "Does Jackie believe in ghosts?" Right at that moment, Jackie walked into the room. When I asked him, he replied ambivalently, "I've never seen any ghosts except in TV series." However, he has been a good sport about things that go bump in the night when I once felt a small child hugging me while sitting on the bed of our hutong house shortly upon moving in; I was a bit scared but felt it was a loving presence. Maybe we are living in a haunted hutong house?

Between Halloween and Christmas, Jackie and I also celebrate our birthdays in autumn. We have always celebrated Jackie's birthday according to the lunar calendar that is widely used in China and mine according to the Western calendar, with birthday cakes. The Chinese make less of a deal out of birthdays than Westerners, but today, cakes are also a part of the celebrations, and you can order elaborate ones at Chinese bakeries and some even surpass their Western counterparts.

Early on in our relationship, Jackie was on a film stint in northeast China during my birthday but had a bit of time to have a cake baked especially for me. On the cake there was an image of a little girl with curly hair. She was dressed in a yellow *qipao* (旗袍), or cheongsam, and was created out of icing; the girl was supposed to resemble me. There was a sweet message written on the cake in Chinese, also with icing: "Happy birthday, Tammy! You are my forever queen." To date, it has been my very favorite birthday cake because of the most important ingredient that went into making it: love.

One of the most memorable birthdays was Jackie's in 2021. There was a multi-sensory Vincent Van Gogh exhibit that featured large LED screens of Van Gogh's paintings, classical music that reflected the moods and various stages of Van Gogh's life, and aroma dispensers. It was a feast of colors with a room full of artificial sunflowers and mirrors in imitation of endless sunflower fields, a recreation of Van Gogh's bedroom, and a sketching tutorial Jackie eagerly participated in. One day, I vowed to myself, I would take Jackie to see some of Van Gogh's original paintings as he had never seen them before and give him another taste of Western bourgeois culture.

Over the years in China, I have also come to enjoy Christmases at the crossroads between East and West. Christmas had always brought up conflicted feelings for me—a sense of nostalgia for the family hearth and yet disdain for its commercial aspect. Yes, I had a love-hate relationship with Christmas, and Beijing made it easier to escape the holiday stress simply because there were really no expectations, emotionally or material-wise, for that festival in Beijing.

One Christmas, I received a book from my parents about the similarities between Christianity and Buddhism. It said that if you are well rooted in your own tradition, you will have an easier time understanding other traditions—a tree with stronger roots will have an easier time absorbing nutrients when it is transplanted into different soil. True.

TAMMY TREICHEL

One year, Jackie and I discovered a Polish Christmas market in the suburbs of Beijing. The scale of the market was modest compared to what I was used to from my days as a student in Heidelberg, Germany, but the taste of mulled wine and the Christmas music brought back some good memories of my socializing with my fellow students outdoors in Heidelberg's historic district beneath the glow of the Christmas lights. I purchased a poinsettia plant, which intrigued Jackie. I explained to him that the red star-shaped plant was a traditional part of Christmas decor in many American homes. It wasn't easy getting poinsettias and real Christmas trees in Beijing; you had to know either where to look or make a lucky discovery.

In fact, Jackie enjoyed the Christmas market so much, he asked me when we were going to our next Christmas event. He had also been actively opening the doors on the advent calendar I had bought him after I explained the notion of counting down the days to Christmas. What's more, I caught him humming "Jingle Bells"; it's a catchy tune many Chinese are familiar with. Where some Western traditions are concerned, however, Jackie is a *tabula rasa*; for example, he thought that reindeer antlers were dragon's horns.

Another Christmas tradition Jackie took to rather quickly was the habit of wearing an "ugly Christmas sweater" as Christmas approaches; this was a natural fit as Jackie loves clothes and fashion accessories. One year, he bought us a pair of matching "ugly Christmas sweaters." When Jackie and I were first dating, he occasionally suggested we wear matching outfits. Interestingly, in the West, this trend doesn't appear quite as popular; maybe because of Westerners' attachment to individuality? Actually, I didn't think the Christmas sweaters Jackie had bought were ugly at all, but quite creative as they featured pictures of different types of cats' heads in baubles. I made a point of attaching a photo of Jackie and me wearing those sweaters in our digital Christmas cards for our friends overseas. The vendor who had sold Jackie the sweaters also used the photo of us modeling the sweaters to advertise them.

Shortly before one of our most recent Christmas celebrations, Jackie came home one day and said, "Close your eyes!" This was vintage Jackie. Since the start of our courtship, he has loved giving me surprises while placing his hands over my eyes. I loved the predictability and stability of his love but also his spontaneous way of expressing it.

"New Year's is coming!" Jackie exclaimed this time. "Last night I was very excited, so today I followed my 第六感 (diliugan). Do you know what that means?"

"Yes!" I replied, smiling. "It's the Chinese word for 'intuition.'"

I opened the shopping bag Jackie had placed on the bed and slowly unpacked the contents—oh wow, many colorful little Christmas baubles! Santa Claus, reindeer, snowman and angel ornaments fashioned into little bells that we could hang on the real Christmas tree I had already ordered online. There was even something among the baubles that Jackie had bought that he thought was a starfish but was actually a Christmas star. I was delighted that Jackie was remembering and appreciating the Western holidays now as well. As someone who usually didn't work with calendars (as opposed to myself), Jackie's intuition was serving him well that yes, Christmas and New Year's were coming!

A rather unique Christmas saw Jackie and me in his home in Yang County, not too far from Xi'an, in 2017. When we arrived at the train station on the new, very punctual high-speed train, we garnered a lot of stares because of the Santa Claus hats we were wearing. Of course, wearing the Santa Claus hats was my idea. We wore the hats all the way to Jackie's home, on the streets and in the taxi.

When we arrived at Jackie's home, his father squinted his eyes and asked, "What is up with those hats you are wearing?" So I tried to explain the concept of Santa Claus to him. I am not sure he understood, but our gifts for the family were gleefully unpacked. Despite globalization, Santa Claus hadn't completely made it to some remote corners of China yet, but I found that Santa Claus as a bearer of gifts and good will was a concept that could be universally understood.

We wrapped up our celebrations with a home-cooked meal accompanied by mulled rice wine, and petted the tiny snow white puppy called Dian Dian (点点), which translates as "Spot" that Jackie's father had recently acquired. The next day, I took Jackie and his mother to a church, and we played it safe with an ensuing visit to a Buddhist temple; after all, Jackie's mother was a Buddhist so we should pay our respects there as well. It was the first time for Jackie and his mother to visit a church, and although we had missed the Christmas celebrations, we were given a tour of the church and beautifully wrapped apples as a gift. The words for *apple* and *peace* sound very similar in Chinese, and Christmas Eve is known as *Pinganye* (平安夜), literally "peaceful evening"; hence, the juxtaposition of apples and Christmas in China.

On a subsequent Christmas in Beijing, I took Jackie to the Xishiku Church (西什库天主堂), also known as the North Church or Church of the Savior, to attend Christmas mass on Christmas Day, as I was raised in the Catholic tradition. After mass, I was amazed at how Jackie was lightning-quick to take a selfie of himself with the Chinese Mother Mary and Baby Jesus figurines in the church. Now I concede that some people might be opposed to taking selfies at a holy site and they might have their good reasons; but there were no signs forbidding it and I thought: a group photo with Mother Mary and Baby Jesus, why not?

I am a searcher and believer in forces greater than ourselves, so yes, perhaps I can identify myself as an occasional believer and "submarine Christian" as a friend of mine once put it (meaning, you emerge and go to church only on major holidays). Jackie is more of an agnostic. "I learned about God from American movies," he once confided to me and said where such matters were concerned, he was fine with following my lead by celebrating Christmas and going to mass once or twice a year.

However, he has never expressed interest in being a full-blown Christian, and I am completely fine with that; people need to come to their own convictions and conclusions. Now if Jackie were a Buddhist, for example, I am sure I might also find myself adopting some of his rituals and perhaps beliefs, who knows? Relationships can open you up to all sorts of possibilities.

Of course, I am aware some people are unwilling to marry someone outside of their traditions and faith, but to me, this was not an issue; in fact, that would be too rigid and unexciting. To me, tolerance and an open mind are more important in a relationship than being bound to any steadfast doctrine.

Jackie and I also combined our Christmas with a bit of charity, because I wanted him to realize that Christmas had to do not only with receiving, but even more, with giving. For example, these last few Christmases we have been dropping off gifts for disadvantaged children under a Christmas tree set up in a café, organized by the Migrant Children's Foundation. "You foreigners are really good," Jackie observed when I first told him about our gift-giving plan. Of course, now that more Chinese people are enjoying some disposable income, I do believe China will gradually see more Chinese people engaging in charity as well.

TAMMY TREICHEL

The similarity I saw between the Spring Festival and Christmas was a yearning for light in the midst of winter, and being together with family in a warm, cozy atmosphere. Yes, the Spring Festival is the Chinese Christmas, and excitement is in the air starting in December and lasting all the way to January or February—the Spring Festival—each year. After all, we all need to keep each other entertained during the cold, dark winter months in northern China.

To me, the Spring Festival, or the Chinese Lunar New Year, which falls in the dead of winter, is grossly misnamed, at least in northern China. The locals in down jackets dance outside in sub-zero temperatures, skate over Beijing's Houhai Lake and draw Chinese characters in the occasional snow. The festival, for Chinese people, is a lot like Christmas and Thanksgiving rolled into one. It's about family reunions, sharing meals, merrymaking and exchanging gifts such as red envelopes stuffed with cash, now often sent digitally via WeChat.

Jackie got into the mood early one year and hid a red envelope with some money in it in our Christmas tree for good luck. Now, if possible, we try to keep our Christmas tree up until the Spring Festival and beyond, even if it starts dropping its needles, so it can do double duty as a kind of Spring Festival tree as well.

Jackie taught me how to write Spring Festival couplets in black ink on red paper for either side of the front door, but the result wasn't aesthetically pleasing at all, so my couplets always landed straight in the trash. Shortly before the Spring Festival, posters go up, forbidding the lighting of fireworks in the city center to prevent fires, injuries and pollution. Parks are also decorated for the temple fairs, and so are houses and office buildings. Red lanterns festoon doorways.

The Spring Festival spirit is contagious, and I caught myself getting into the spirit as well. Being immersed in a totally different culture means you can "piggyback" and enjoy the local festivals with the locals—in my case now, Jackie. On the eve of the Spring Festival after my return to China in 2015, there were still a lot of fireworks outside in the Yonghegong neighborhood; an expat friend had warned me that Beijing around New Year's was like a "war zone." I caught Jackie enthusiastically yelling, "China is crazy!" in heavily accented English while filming himself with fireworks in the background. Now, several years later, absolutely no fireworks are being set off at Yonghegong due to safety reasons. What remains unchanged, however, is that many shops and restaurants are closed during that period, with China being paralyzed for a week or more when there is a mass migration of people to visit families in their hometowns.

But not everyone is making and feeling merry during the Spring Festival. Some expats find themselves either lonely or bored as their Chinese friends celebrate with families. An American friend of mine had a Grinch-like attitude toward the Spring Festival as it delayed work on his start-up company. "Hate holiday... slowdown not fun," he messaged me. My attitude toward the festival also soured on occasion as deliveries were significantly delayed and some of my late-night commutes home from work were fraught with immense difficulty as it was hard getting a taxi; this was before I discovered the previously mentioned night bus and its adventures.

What's positive is that I have now—thanks to Jackie—developed a strong enthusiasm for Beijing's New Year's markets, which open in the weeks before Spring Festival and are either held indoors or outdoors. If it weren't for Jackie, I am sure I wouldn't have discovered them. At the markets, you can buy meats, wine, tea, snacks, decorations and other goods for personal consumption or as gifts for the Chinese New Year. At one market, the vendors came from different provinces in

China, and I also spotted foreigners from Eastern Europe, the Middle East and Africa hawking their goods—Eastern European chocolates and wines, Persian rugs of modest quality and prices, and beautifully carved African furniture.

When Jackie and I went together to prepare for our Spring Festival celebrations, we bought preserved meat, vinegar, mulled rice wine, decorations and bundles of winter sweet branches that would bloom once you place them in water. Jackie greatly enjoyed going to the markets, and one of the reasons was the free samples of food, which he said would allow him to eat his fill right on the spot.

For my part, I was into sampling the different kinds of liquor, and even got a buzz before we left the market. Better yet, a box of cured meat has arrived regularly for Spring Festival every year via mail from Jackie's parents in Yang County as well, more delicious than you could buy at any market; Jackie said his parents had prepared the meat themselves. One year, he hung a large cured fish from his father on the laundry rack in our small courtyard, out of reach of the jaws of hungry neighborhood cats and weasels that haunt the hutongs, until we were ready to consume it.

To celebrate the Year of the Dog, Jackie and I were invited to the Beijing TV (BTV) New Year's Gala through the kindness of one of my coworkers. We had VIP-style seats at a table in the front row, and we enjoyed various song and dance shows by some top Chinese performers. Many Chinese attending hoped that they would be caught laughing or clapping on camera when it panned into the audience and then also appear on the show vicariously when it aired. Frankly, I couldn't care less whether I appeared on camera as an enthusiastic audience member; I just came to wholeheartedly enjoy the performance and atmosphere. Thus it didn't come as a surprise that I didn't make it on the final cut. But Jackie, a natural in front of the camera, did for a second or so, laughing and clapping at some slapstick skit.

Then there is the Western Valentine's Day on February 14 and Chinese Valentine's Day, or Qixi (七夕), which falls on a different date every year according to the lunar calendar, in late summer. Despite many Chinese being very pragmatic when it comes to matters of the heart—apartments, cars and stable careers are frequently prerequisites for marriage, as well as occasionally, the paying of controversial "bride prices" (money paid by the groom's family to the bride's family upon marriage)—Chinese culture can also cater to us romantics.

Think of the Butterfly Lovers (梁祝), also known as China's Romeo and Juliet, and the Cowherd and the Weaver Girl (牛郎织女). The Qixi Festival, also known as the Double Seventh Festival, is so named because it falls on the seventh day of the seventh lunar month. The festival is rooted in the most romantic myth: The Cowherd (牛郎) and the Weaver Girl (织女) are lovers separated by a river of stars because love between a goddess and a mortal was not allowed. But once a year, magpies take pity on the separated lovers and form a bridge so they can be reunited for one night. In myth, as opposed to real life mostly, absence makes the heart grow fonder, it seems. The Cowherd is represented by the star Altair and the Weaver Girl by Vega, while the Milky Way represents the river separating them.

There have been many traditions linked to this old tale in the past. Today, young Chinese couples like to exchange gifts such as chocolates and flowers on Qixi or enjoy a romantic meal together—so, quite like the Western Valentine's Day it has been commercialized. Some even choose it as their wedding day. I enjoy both Chinese and Western festivals as I can also "cash in" and express my love to Jackie on both holidays; the same applies to Jackie. Jackie and I like to go to bakeries or cafés for a rendezvous or give each other little gifts on these holidays — items of clothing or body products.

The most romantic gift to date, however, was when Jackie was working in Sydney, Australia for several months in 2016. I missed Jackie. He was working on a Jackie Chan movie, but despite being half a world away, he didn't forget Qixi. He made a bilingual poster featuring a photo of both of us reading "宝贝我爱你 ~ Baby I love you ~ 七夕快乐 ~ Happy Chinese Valentine's Day." The English words were a bit wobbly, but whimsical because Jackie usually doesn't write in English; the penmanship was somewhat like a schoolboy's, but the Chinese characters were bold, clear and beautiful to me. The 七夕快乐 almost isn't legible anymore because it was written in pale pink, but traces of the words are still there if you look closely.

Jackie found locals at a Sydney supermarket, and asked them to hold up the sign so he could take photos of them with his homemade poster. As he can't speak English fluently, he wrote his request on the back of the sign: "Can you help me with a shadow [*sic*, photo]. My girlfriend works in Beijing, China. I want to give her a surprise. Today is the Chinese Valentine's Day."

I am not sure whether he got help composing those instructions in English from someone in his acting crew, or whether he did some research to find the right English words. The excitement of being in a foreign country for the first time in his life in his thirties was written on Jackie's face in the photos, and I was happy to see his happiness. That to me was part of the gift he gave me on Qixi.

8

"Beijing is your oyster"

Jackie and I feel very much at home in our Yonghegong neighborhood, which has seen quite a few changes in the past few years. We used to visit the underground vegetable market at Ditan Park but it has since closed. A lot of buildings in the hutongs have been bricked up in a drive for gentrification. The hutongs have gotten a cleaner and more uniform appearance, but they now look like something out of Universal Studios or Disney, namely fake-looking edifices, instead of actual houses inhabited by living and breathing inhabitants with inevitable building quirks.

I miss the original, occasionally bohemian appearance of our neighborhood and believe it has lost a significant amount of its charm, but Jackie appears to be enjoying our new ambience because he thinks it looks like a film set. I have found many Chinese like Jackie to be remarkably resilient and adaptive, traits they need to develop in order to survive the rapid changes China is undergoing.

For example, Jackie and I liked to frequent a small mom-and-pop store run by an elderly couple in our hutong. To comply with new building requirements, they had to modify their hutong house and convert the front door into a window. So instead of walking directly into their store to buy our water or vinegar, we knocked on the window and conducted our business through it. It was now sort of like a McDonald's drive-through you would see in the US. The dumpling-making workshop run by our neighbor Joyce experienced (no "has") a similar treatment; her former front door was bricked up and converted into a small window, and the building could be accessed from the side only.

Someone who has not been affected by the cosmetic surgery in our neighborhood so far is the hairdresser Jackie and I frequent. Our hairdresser said she has been in the same little no-frills shop for ten-plus years and her store front has not experienced any changes since we moved into the neighborhood several years ago. I love practicing Chinese with her and she does a good job of giving Jackie and me haircuts at very reasonable rates.

Getting a good haircut in China can be a challenge for foreigners because of the finer texture of Western hair, whereas Asians experience the same problem in the West, but our hairdresser is a pro at both. However, if Jackie and I are pressed for time, we visit itinerant haircutters who do business in parks behind bamboo shrubs or under bridges as long as they aren't being chased away by security guards. The going rate when I last checked was 10 yuan (roughly USD 1.50).

This brings to mind the only time I remember ever being really angry at Jackie, and it involved his hair and our hairdresser. One evening, I came home from work. As I was taking off my light coat — it was the beginning of May — and about to hang it on our coat rack, Jackie came to greet me. When we greet each other or are very happy, we occasionally engage in "Eskimo kisses" with my big nose rubbing against his small one and take in each other's scent – but not this time! I glanced at Jackie, did a double take, dropped my coat in shock and threw up my arms. I was starting to feel like the proverbial bull in a china shop.

"Jackie… Jackie… what… whatever happened to your hair?" I stuttered, my heart pounding.

There was my Jackie, with his beautiful raven-black hair all shorn off!

"I got a role in a movie. A big movie. Although it is a small role, I still want to play it," Jackie confessed, suddenly shy and avoiding looking me in the eye. I learned Jackie had been recruited to play an air force officer in a patriotic blockbuster and the role required a shaved head.

"Your beautiful black hair!" I stormed. I truly thought I was about to go stark raving mad! I really loved Jackie's hair, it was so lush and attractive, and I loved running my hands through it to feel its rich silky texture and smell its fine natural oil. For a brief second, I contemplated the crazy idea of rushing to the hairdresser's to collect Jackie's hair with a broom and dustpan and glue the hairs onto a kind of hairnet and make Jackie a wig, or buy a wig that looked like Jackie's original hair online and have him wear that until his hair had grown back.

"Jackie, did you ever consider that I am also your audience?" I asked him. Jackie slunk off, sulking. We didn't really talk for a day or two, and for the next two months Jackie hid his shorn head under a changing array of baseball caps, a new look he would start to relish while his hair was growing back.

After browsing for men's wigs on the shopping platform Taobao, I decided a wig wouldn't restore Jackie's natural look. I turned to WeChat and texted our hairdresser. In diplomatic terms, I told her in my best Chinese that I thought Jackie's new haircut was a complete disaster.

"Excuse me... what happened to Jackie's hair?" I texted as an opener.

"Haha... he chose the style himself," our hairdresser texted back.

"Thanks... I know you were doing your job, but I don't like it."

"Okay... Just understand, I need to respect my customers' wishes," she replied. "Everyone is entitled to their own opinion."

That was true. Our hairdresser kindly comforted me, and assured me that Jackie's hair would grow back quickly, especially as summer was around the corner. She even suggested that Jackie get more rest and eat nutritious foods so his hair would grow back quicker. And grow back Jackie's hair did after he had played his movie role, thank heavens, lusher and more beautiful than ever!

Almost every day for two months, I would gently lift Jackie's baseball cap and check whether his hair had grown another millimeter. In the end, we decided he would get the sides of his head shaved occasionally so that he would have an easier time landing certain film roles, e.g., policemen or soldiers, or security guards. If it was a Qing-dynasty movie requiring shaved heads instead of wigs, we would give it a pass. Indeed, compromise and understanding are key in any relationship.

I believe one of the best pieces of relationship/marriage advice my father gave me was over a glass of wine (his marriage to my mother saw its 40th anniversary before his death): Compromise makes a marriage work; if only one partner gets his or her way, it will eventually sow the seeds of conflict.

I kept this advice in mind when I fell in love with a retro rose wallpaper pattern and was eager to cover both sides of one door in our hutong house with it. Jackie agreed I cover one side of the door with the wallpaper, namely the side I always saw first thing in the morning when I woke up, but he preferred to leave the door on the living room side white. Fair enough. After all, the home is a microcosm and home decisions reflect major life decisions on a much smaller scale.

But back to our neighborhood. There is a nearby shop that specializes in *qipaos* and has survived the changes in our neighborhood in the last couple of years. I don't know exactly when my love affair with qipaos started. I just know I was smitten when Jackie and I saw Chinese actresses wearing qipaos in the 2001 TV series *Romance in the Rain* (情深深雨濛濛), which is set in 1930s Shanghai. Jackie's favorite actress in a supporting role was Li Yu (李钰 or Cindy Lee) because of her smart, tomboyish look in a qipao.

The exact origin of the qipao is up for debate, with some saying it originated from a one-piece dress of Manchu origin in the Qing dynasty, while others trace it to Western influences. The qipao became popular in the 1920s and 1930s, when it became a symbol of women's liberation. After being out of fashion for several decades due to the political turbulence that followed the communist victory in 1949, the qipao has again become selectively fashionable in recent decades.

Some Chinese ladies today like to wear qipaos for special events, e.g., red ones for weddings, or if their children are about to take the college entrance exam because they believe a qipao will bring good luck. I wear them more frequently. To me, this classic article of clothing is the most gorgeous of all kinds of dresses, not because of what a qipao reveals, but because of what it conceals.

I have several qipaos in my wardrobe, some of them bought at the shop not too far from our home. The most recent qipao was a much-treasured gift from Jackie—a pistachio-colored real silk qipao with yellow birds sitting rather gleefully in persimmon trees and orange knotted buttons on it, quite an unusual color combination. Jackie had gotten a better price for it after the shopkeeper on duty asked him to recite the words "阿弥陀佛" ("*Amituo Fo*"), a Buddhist prayer, ten times. Perhaps this was bargaining, Yonghegong-style?

The average foreigner's body build differs from that of Chinese—many foreign women are larger and curvier, which makes it hard for some foreigners to pull off the qipao look. Yet qipaos sit very well on other foreigners, for example American actress Grace Kelly, who looked very convincing in one. Because I am not too short, at least by Chinese standards, and pretty slim, I can usually buy qipaos off the rack, and they don't look that bad on me.

In the US, non-Asians are sometimes criticized on social media for wearing qipaos because of so-called "cultural appropriation" but in China, people have a more reasonable and open-minded approach: If foreigners wear qipaos, it is seen as a gesture of appreciation for Chinese culture.

Ah, traditional Chinese culture! Jackie has often accompanied me on my discovery journey, and together, we have checked out the typical tourist attractions in Beijing such as the Forbidden City and Summer Palace, as well as the Great Wall at Badaling, and took a bicycle rickshaw ride through the old hutongs near Prince Gong's mansion (such rides are usually offered at ridiculously extravagant prices, so *caveat emptor*). Of these attractions, Jackie had always been very eager to see the Forbidden City and the Great Wall, unarguably Beijing's most famous attractions. As a *beipiao*, however, he was always either working or looking for work, so he never had time. Therefore, he had vowed to visit these two sites once he had a girlfriend—and when I came along, so did the opportunity.

Jackie and I also explored different former residences of famous people, e.g., the homes of writer Lu Xun (鲁迅), the "red" Soong sister, Song Qingling (宋庆龄), artist Qi Baishi (齐白石), who is known for his whimsical watercolors and Peking opera star Mei Lanfang (梅兰芳), whose claim to fame was playing female or 旦 (*dan*) leading roles and who introduced his highly sophisticated craft of Peking opera to foreign countries, including the US. Jackie and I were in seventh heaven viewing the relics associated with these historical figures, inhaling the musty smell of their former homes, and admiring the old, gnarled trees in the courtyards, which had witnessed these people at work, relaxing or going about mundane activities. And all of these things could be found right under our noses, in our backyard.

When I first moved to Beijing, an American friend and seasoned expat sent me a welcome email proclaiming, "Beijing is your oyster. Meaning it's yours to explore and do with what you want. There are pearls if you look with open eyes." And pearls I did find, with Jackie's help. Actually, the oyster's greatest gift is Jackie himself.

The two of us eventually extended our radius and visited the Beijing outskirts. Traveling in China is relatively safe, but I make a point of not traveling alone outside Beijing as a foreign woman. I am able to ask for directions, book train tickets and check into hotels by myself, but I prefer to travel with a Chinese companion, first and foremost, Jackie. They can help negotiate the best deals and may make you appear more approachable to the locals.

Another one of our forays into traditional Chinese culture involved an excursion to the home of a calligraphy master, who lived way out in the suburbs. Next to qipaos, I am crazy about Chinese paintings and am slowly warming to calligraphy.

Some women may spend their hard-earned money on designer clothes, shoes and makeup, but I have spent it on a painting with avant-garde plum blossoms, or a misty Yellow Mountain scene in autumn, as well as a freezing monkey clasping some fruit and what looks like a limping rooster for which I cut out and glued on a paper crutch at Jackie's request as he is sensitive to detail.

So when a Chinese calligraphy master I had met at an event invited Jackie and me to his studio, I was excited. My limited exposure to calligraphy in the past consisted of strolling through the National Art Museum of China or admiring elderly men painting characters on Beijing's sidewalks with large brushes, buckets of water and a few flicks of the wrist.

Calligraphy master and painter Wang Xing (王星) is an internationally renowned artist who has won first prizes for his talent. In China, calligraphy is sometimes used for certain brands as a logo, and I was surprised to learn the calligraphy on the Thirteen Spices Powder (十三香) packaging is his; he had also designed the box. Thirteen Spices Powder is a staple in Chinese kitchens and is also found in our hutong house kitchen.

Calligraphy and painting are very much related — after all, Chinese characters originated from pictographs. To me, and I assume many other foreigners, calligraphy is harder to appreciate than Chinese paintings because the paintings show something concrete, while calligraphy is abstract, apparently made up of random brush strokes.

Master Wang's spacious apartment in the outskirts of Beijing doubles as a studio, where he engages in calligraphy and paints.

HUTONG HEARTTHROBS

The living room had a long table featuring the "four treasures of the study" — brushes, ink stone, ink stick and paper. He invited Jackie and me to practice calligraphy, the repetition of which is considered a form of meditation, but we politely declined. My forays into the calligraphy world were limited to the Chinese Spring Festival and only produced scribbles.

Master Wang asked me what characters I wished to have him write and we settled on 随缘 (*suiyuan*), meaning "according to fate" — such a simple yet weighty expression said to determine so much of what happens in life. He produced the characters with a few masterstrokes. I thought it was a suitable choice for someone like me who likes to ponder weighty topics such as the rather opaque Chinese concept of *yuanfen* — fate which brings two or more people together.

Traditional Chinese painting has at least two major subjects, flowers and birds (花鸟 or *huaniao*), which includes other animals and plants, and landscapes (山水 or *shanshui*). Master Wang told me he was focusing on landscapes, exemplified by his *magnum opus*, a seven-meter long scroll of the Great Wall to be exhibited in a national museum. It was breathtakingly beautiful, featuring hardly a trace of human activity on the man-made wall.

It reminded me of the Song-dynasty (AD 960 - AD 1279) panoramic painting *Along the River During the Qingming Festival* (清明上河图) that features more than 800 people from different social strata in miniature going about their daily activities during a spring day; that painting is as famous in China as the *Mona Lisa* in the West. Master Wang had been working on his Great Wall painting for three years and it was far from finished. Someone had offered to buy it for a stupendous sum of money, but he refused to part with the painting as he wanted to donate it to the museum.

Master Wang appeared to have a very healthy constitution.

Was it perhaps because he ate apples every day from the neighboring orchard? Or maybe it was the calligraphy that was keeping him healthy? Like meditation, calligraphy is said to have health benefits such as stress reduction and it is said calligraphers enjoy a long life.

Be that as it may, one thing was certain: Master Wang believed he knew the key to a successful life. "Only do one thing and do it well is the secret to success," he told us.

Also in the suburbs of Beijing, Jackie arranged for me to attend the taping of a segment of the TV show *Mom's Bible* (拜托了妈妈) one summer, as he knew one of the people who managed the program. The TV host, Ms. Li Jing (李静), is a household name in China.

I sat in the front row; the audience, all Chinese moms except for me. Many Chinese ladies in the audience were beautifully dressed, and I spotted one woman even wearing a qipao. Similarly to the audience members of the BTV gala, the aim of many of these women was no doubt to be shown on TV and even better yet, be chosen to comment using a microphone.

I enjoyed the suspense as the Chinese moms all swayed their plastic roses to the beat of the program's music. *Mom's Bible* was, of course, another excellent opportunity to practice my Chinese comprehension skills and understand Chinese culture better. The topics of the program were: Should you turn on the air conditioning in the summer for your children or use other means to stay cool? What are the symptoms of a heat stroke and how can you avoid them in children? What kinds of fruits and vegetables are the best for your children? Surveys were then conducted via smart phones.

I was relieved I wasn't asked to comment as I felt self-conscious about my Chinese and didn't have anything of value to contribute to the topics being discussed. However, I enjoyed watching the program's anchor Li Jing at work; I liked her energy. Li Jing has been called a "daredevil anchor woman" because she is known for her casual style on air and does not shy away from asking provocative questions.

During the program, they showed a film clip of an American mother locking her toddler in a hot car and going shopping. The cherubic child suffers a heatstroke, and luckily some shoppers take notice, break into the car and call the paramedics. Statistics were presented on how many children die each year of heatstroke (you hear a lot about this in American news; I am not sure how it is in China). The audience gasped with outrage at the mother's negligence.

After the clip, Li Jing appeared to be critical of Western parents, asking in Chinese, "Who is taking care of whom?" Without a doubt, leaving a child in a hot car is grossly negligent and bound to trigger outrage. But, of course, suggesting that all Western family units lack responsibility, caring and cohesion would be going too far.

In general, notwithstanding individual differences, it is my impression that Chinese parents are very much involved in their children's lives, make a lot of sacrifices for them and build their lives around them. It's hands-on parenting, even when their children have grown up. Meanwhile, many Western parents like my mother tend to foster independence in their children, give them a lot of space to make their own discoveries and draw their own conclusions, and have more of a hands-off parenting approach.

I didn't really learn anything completely new on the program, but I greatly appreciated the opportunity to see this legendary TV chat show host at work, get a glimpse into what questions occupy Chinese parents, and of course learn a little bit more about how Chinese view Westerners. It also helped me ponder some differences between Chinese and Western parents and families.

———∞———

Beyond Beijing's outskirts in neighboring Hebei province, there is the Chengde Imperial Mountain Resort, where the Qing-dynasty emperors kept cool during the summer, the picturesque Old Dragon's Head where the Great Wall meets the sea, and the Beidaihe summer resort, which was Jackie's first time at the beach and on a boat. Fortunately, he did not get seasick although he does on occasion get a bit car sick.

We couldn't go swimming because the water was too cold in June. Plus, Jackie, like many Chinese who had grown up in the countryside, couldn't swim, so I made sure he was wearing a life jacket when we boarded the boat. We enjoyed the seaside with its salty air, sea shells and seafood. We rented two beach chairs and an umbrella, took some breaths of fresh air, relaxed and enjoyed the view.

The next year, however, Jackie and I finally got the chance to go swimming at Moon Island (月坨岛), a small resort island named after its shape of a crescent moon. Jackie went "swimming" for the first time in his life (in his thirties, no less), and I kept a watchful eye on him, although there were lifeguards on duty. By "swimming," I mean we had a great time splashing around and soaking in the waist-deep salt water of the Bohai Sea near the shore. When Jackie once showed me a photo of himself beside the majestic Sydney Harbor, he admitted to me, pointing to the water: "It makes me afraid."

There were fewer people on Moon Island than at Beidaihe, it seemed, and as it was far less developed, you could find some quiet pockets in which to enjoy nature, which features abundant plant and bird life. Some people went fishing or crabbing or enjoyed the hot springs there. We lived in a Dutch-style wooden house, or rather, a kind of Venetian house on stilts, which was lit up at night by strings of colorful lights strung across the eaves.

The house swayed gently if the inhabitants made heavy movements, which unnerved Jackie a bit but soothed me as it was like the rocking of a cradle. After all, we badly needed a getaway from our hutong house from time to time, as endearing as it was. Before turning in, I evicted a big spider that was hiding underneath the bed cover. Jackie and I slept soundly and had a very relaxing getaway close to the natural elements—water, sun, salt, sand. Definitely money well spent for urbanites who wanted to enjoy a whiff of nature and get away from the crowds and stress of daily city life.

Another attraction in Hebei province was Rongguofu, a complex of buildings in the city of Shijiazhuang built expressly for the filming of the famous Chinese TV series *Dream of the Red Chamber*. Of course, Jackie came with me for this excursion. The series, based on the eponymous novel (also known as *A Dream of Red Mansions* or *The Story of the Stone*; in Chinese 红楼梦), was released in 1987. The novel, written during the mid-18th century, tells the story of the noble Jia (贾) family at its peak, the love triangle between Jia Baoyu and his two cousins—and the clan's downfall.

It is one of China's four classic novels, along with *Romance of the Three Kingdoms*, *Journey to the West* and *Water Margin*. We couldn't resist buying *Dream of the Red Chamber* film posters. Upon returning home, Jackie was initially reluctant about my hanging up these posters because of the film's tragic love story. On occasion, I am more superstitious than Jackie, e.g., I avoid walking under ladders or opening a black umbrella indoors, but Jackie has his moments.

Shijiazhuang is also home to the Hebei Museum, which

features a fine collection of china and artifacts. Jackie got all excited about it and talked about wanting to see the ancient "clothes" there that he remembered seeing in his school history books. To me, Jackie was like a sphinx, talking in riddles—what did he mean by the Chinese word for "clothes"? Clothes cannot really survive over centuries!

It turned out he was referring to the jade-plated burial suits of a royal couple in the Han dynasty (206 BC - AD 220), sort of like "his and hers" outfits made for eternity—I had also seen photos of the gorgeous burial suits during an East Asian history course in Heidelberg. Jackie continued to talk animatedly about the burial suits even after our museum visit. Perhaps we should also acquire a pair of matching burial suits when our time comes, I thought with amusement.

Not far away in Tianjin, Jackie and I marveled at the rather grotesque Porcelain House, which is almost completely decorated with porcelain shards. Lonely Planet called it Tianjin's "tackiest sight by a long shot" and an "ode to both porcelain and questionable taste." We also visited the home of the Empress Dowager Cixi's lady-in-waiting Der Ling (德龄), who wrote about the inner workings of the Qing-dynasty Manchu court in her memoir *Two Years in the Forbidden City*, in which—as opposed to many other rather negative accounts of the Empress Dowager—she portrayed Cixi in a rather favorable light.

Jackie then showed me around the last Emperor Puyi's former residence in Tianjin, Jingyuan Garden, where Jackie had participated in a film shoot playing a military officer.

Near Tianjin proper is a district called Jizhou (蓟州), where there are many wonderful sights to visit—old temples, a karst cave, Mount Pan, which the Qing-dynasty Emperor Qianlong visited thirty-two times and wrote more than one thousand poems about, and my favorite destination there, White Snake

Valley (白蛇谷).

One April, Jackie and I went hiking in White Snake Valley, which did not appear to shelter snakes, let alone white ones, but definitely did have tiny lizards that were sunbathing when we were there. The air was fresh, and the wind whistled through the birches on the mountain sides. The paths were at times narrow and steep and Jackie took photos of us visibly nervous as we clutched at the metal chains that served as stair rails. Jackie displayed a daredevil attitude, but I urged caution as I didn't want twisted ankles or broken bones, especially in a remote place where help was far away. At the end of the day, we had survived the thrills of White Snake Valley, but our calves hurt from the steep ascent and ensuing descent.

The place is named after Madame White Snake, who according to a Chinese legend, went there to study before moving to Hangzhou and marrying a mortal herb doctor called Xu Xian (许仙). "Madame White Snake" is my favorite Chinese fairytale because next to being a charming love story about an immortal-in-the-making-meets-mortal, it deals with the themes of mortality and immortality. Anyhow, eternal life is also an Easter theme, and we happened to be there on Easter Sunday.

In White Snake Valley, Jackie and I went hiking for six kilometers and saw remnants of the Great Wall in the distance. We also went to the White Snake temple and lit some incense; after all, the snake is my totem. The temple was in a cave, and you could see a stone snake head in the back on the cave wall.

The monk there was pretty feisty and business-minded, trying to sell us deluxe incense sticks. When Jackie told him I was born in the Year of the Snake, he advised me to put 60 yuan (about USD 8) into the donation box, as the word for the number six in Chinese sounds similar to the word for "smooth."

9

My "Leading Man" in China

Jackie has been my steadfast travel companion here in China, my "leading man" when it comes to travel and other matters in China, so to say.

One trip took us to Luoyang, Henan province, as the Longmen Grottoes are quite famous and April is the peak season for peonies, China's national flower. We got a rather mixed welcome there. The dearth of foreigners made the locals and Chinese tourists in Luoyang, a third-tier city, more curious about people like me, with some children giggling and shouting "外国

人" (*waiguoren* means "foreigner") behind my back. Some people were more fascinated by my travel companion. One tourist, a middle-aged lady, exclaimed about Jackie, "Oh, he is handsome! Is he your boyfriend?" When I replied in the affirmative, she said, "Handsome! Look at his lips, just like a bird's!"

That same spring, only a month before, Jackie and I had visited Xi'an for the first time and this was Jackie's turf, close to his hometown. The discovery of the Terracotta Warriors in 1974 was hailed as one of the most stupendous archaeological finds of the 20th century. Emperor Qin Shi Huang (秦始皇) had commissioned these figures to be buried with him in 210 BC-209 BC to protect him in the afterlife. At the Terracotta Warriors, Jackie and I stole a kiss. Would a public display of affection, or PDA, in a necropolis be considered appropriate?

Near Xi'an, Jackie and I also visited the Huaqing Baths (华清池), which are famous for the legendary love story between Emperor Xuanzong (唐玄宗) and his doomed concubine Yang Guifei (楊貴妃) in the Tang dynasty (AD 618 - AD 907). The emperor was besotted with his concubine, one of China's four classic beauties, and neglected his kingdom because of her. She lost her life and he lost his power to rivals because of her.

In their serene days, Emperor Xuanzong had a pool shaped like a crab apple blossom built for Yang Guifei. It was a very romantic getaway for Jackie and me, and we held hands while strolling through the grounds. I thought to myself, chuckling, that once Jackie learned how to swim, I would have a crab apple flower-shaped pool built for him.

Next to Qin Shi Huang's tomb, Jackie suggested we visit the tomb complex of Wu Zetian (武则天), China's only empress, a site called Qianling (乾陵). The mausoleum has for the most part not been excavated, just as Qin Shi Huang's; the mausoleum complex houses the remains of various members of the imperial family of the Tang dynasty, which is regarded as a golden era in Chinese history. Visitors can go underground and view some parts of the tombs that feature murals depicting Tang-dynasty life. I was surprised there was no protective glass on the murals, but maybe they had been covered with a protective varnish as I saw that many Chinese visitors just brushed their hands over the murals. Jackie and I kept our hands in our pockets; our eyes were sufficient to take in the exquisite sights.

After our sojourn in Shaanxi province, we left for Henan and 1,500-year-old Shaolin Monastery (少林寺), which is world-famous for its kung fu. Jackie with his engaging personality soon chatted up one of the monks who agreed to give us a special informational tour of the monastery. Jackie was sincerely interested, as kung fu skills are in demand for some movie roles.

Shaolin Monastery is a magnet for kung fu aficionados. Think of the movie *Kung Fu Panda*, of the larger-than-life martial arts masters Jet Li and Bruce Lee, who combined philosophy with martial arts, and of course Jackie Chan — kung fu is one of China's most successful cultural exports to the West. At home, Jackie and I would later enjoy the 2008 Chinese TV series *The Legend of Bruce Lee* (李小龙传奇), and Jackie had fun pointing out the various foreign actors in the series to me who played extras and were at that time actually students at the Guangdong University of Foreign Studies, where he had worked as a security guard.

When I asked Jackie why he loved kung fu, he simply said, "Kung fu is full of feeling."

As luck would have it, two monks gave us a personal tour. One of them wore a slate-colored robe and did most of the talking, while the other one, the one Jackie had first encountered, sat by quietly in a saffron-colored robe. Both had a very solemn, other-worldly air. The one with the slate-colored robe and glittering, pebble-like eyes said kung fu should be practiced "as a means to understand yourself." Yet he also said many people were misguided and studied it for the wrong reasons, namely to defeat other people. He said one's biggest enemy is oneself, which sounded like a movie line.

When we said goodbye to the monks, I extended my hand but they didn't shake it—my gesture was considered inappropriate, I learned; I should have folded my hands and bowed.

When I emerged from the monastery, I had arrived at the simple yet profound understanding that kung fu is not just about demonstrating some deft moves, but a philosophy and way of life that are cultivated both inside and outside of Shaolin's walls.

Some time later, we took a cruise on the Yangtze River and through the Three Gorges. The ship was swarming with tourists; many of us were leaning over the railings in awe. Jackie and I had booked the most expensive seats, and we were stunned as the panorama of the Xiling Gorge (西陵峡) passed us by, lush vegetation on the peaks and teal waters of the Yangtze. From Yichang, our ship sailed through the Xiling Gorge and on towards the Three Gorges Dam.

The Three Gorges Dam was built for flood control, power generation, and to facilitate shipping, and is the world's largest hydroelectric power station in terms of generating capacity. But many ancient relics and archaeological sites were destroyed as a result of its construction, much natural beauty was erased and 1.3 million people were displaced. Construction on the record-breaking Three Gorges Dam started in 1994 and the project was completed in stages over the next couple of years. Today, there is a five-stage ship lock through which ships can pass, the largest in the world. The ship lift, which we took on our cruise, is a water elevator which can handle a three thousand-ton passenger ship at one time in roughly forty minutes.

We combined the Three Gorges with a lesser known jewel on

our itinerary—Bailihuang (百里黄). When Jackie and I booked a guided tour there at a travel agency next to the Yichang high-speed train station, the agent smiled when Jackie said I was from the US and had come all the way from Beijing to see the famous hawthorn tree from Zhang Yimou's (张艺谋) 2010 film *Under the Hawthorn Tree* (山楂树之恋) in Bailihuang.

Bailihuang advertises itself as "alpine grasslands," and Zhang Yimou shot some scenes there from *Under the Hawthorn Tree*. The understated movie, with its universal themes of waiting, love, loss and innocence, as well as delicate symbolism, left a profound impression on me and I consider it one of my favorite Chinese movies, as does Jackie. It was May and the hawthorn tree that had been used in the movie was in full bloom when we arrived. Birds alighted in the tree, and bees buzzed around the fragrant white flowers with their heavy, honey-like fragrance.

After our visit to the tree, we went to an outdoor go-kart track at Bailihuang to rent a go-kart, with Jackie indicating that I would drive it. The track manager was skeptical. "Can she drive?" he asked Jackie rather sassily, with his hands on his hips. "Of course!" Jackie replied confidently. "She is American. All Americans can drive." That seemed to satisfy the track manager and we were given a go-kart and helmets, and after strapping ourselves into our seats I had a great time speeding around the curves, grinning wickedly, with Jackie hanging on for dear life.

To date, I have visited Jackie's home in Yang County, Shaanxi province, three times. His parents used to be farmers. Before our first visit, Jackie's father asked Jackie over the phone, "What color is your girlfriend's hair?"

"It isn't black, it isn't blond, it also isn't red... it's a mix," Jackie replied. "You'll see once she comes."

HUTONG HEARTTHROBS

His parents were very happy to see us, but unsurprisingly, it was somewhat difficult for me to communicate as they spoke the local dialect with each other, not Mandarin, therefore Jackie had to translate a lot into Mandarin so I could understand. Meanwhile, Jackie's sister, like Jackie, spoke Mandarin slowly and clearly with me, so we had no problem communicating.

During my visits, I was also introduced to Jackie's other family members — it seemed to me he was related to half the people in the county, there were so many relatives to meet — and some friends, and I flipped through old family albums and admired some of Jackie's father's antiques and memorabilia from Jackie's younger years. Among these, what impressed me the most were the characters Jackie had carved into an old wooden table as a student and a poster showing Stefanie Sun (Sun Yanzi, 孙燕姿), a tomboyish Singaporean singer-songwriter whose songs Jackie liked to listen to during his teen years.

I also passed the elementary and middle schools Jackie had attended, which we reached by walking through streets that had racks of long noodles drying in the sun (Shaanxi province is known for its noodle specialties). On one of our strolls, we chanced upon a bustling countryside outdoor wedding, with people eating at tables set up along a street. Relatives, friends and neighbors pitched in to wash the dishes on the street curb afterwards. Indeed, food takes center stage at a Chinese wedding. When Jackie and I watched Meghan Markle's and Prince Harry's televised church wedding in 2018, Jackie remarked, "It's a touching wedding, but where is the food?"

I also vividly remember a visit to a man Jackie called his "干爸" (*ganba*), meaning a secular kind of godfather. He had us sit down in his home illuminated by murky electric lights and offered me some raw beaten eggs with sugar. I wasn't surprised at this offer. During World War II, my father and his family had the same dish as a dessert, salmonella notwithstanding, and I had also eaten it as a child.

During our visit to Jackie's "godfather," Jackie's mother, a vigorous and sociable woman, and I went outside together in the pitch black of night to the outhouse, situated behind the cabbage patches; their home had no indoor plumbing. Restroom breaks are always a good opportunity for ladies to bond, no matter what the conditions. Jackie's mother told me that whatever Jackie and I wanted to do, wherever we wanted to live, worked for her. She reminded me of my American mother, who had cheered on my relationship with Jackie by saying, "If you think Jackie is the man for you, by all means go for it!"

Meanwhile, compared to Jackie's mother, Jackie's father was more reserved and cautious, old school, but with a gentle demeanor, not unlike that of my own father. Also like my father, he wanted his children closer to home. In fact, if my father were still alive, I wonder what he would have thought of Jackie's colorful character. He might have preferred his daughter to be paired off with a white-collar office worker in the US instead of an artist type in faraway China. Yet he might have come around after the initial shock of his daughter being involved with a former Chinese security guard-turned-actor after seeing that she was happy. Who knows?

Now Jackie's father had always had a puppy or two at his side when I visited; Jackie said it was because his father missed him and hoped his son would be closer. When Jackie's father first learned Jackie and I were an item, he sighed and exclaimed, "Too far." Whether he meant too far geographically, culturally, socio-economically or all three, I am not sure, but now he is resigned to the fact that I am a presence in Jackie's life, and perhaps he is also occasionally appreciative, because he knows Jackie and I help and encourage each other in Beijing. After all, you can't argue with good old *yuanfen*, or fate.

In fact, when Jackie was a boy, a fortune teller had passed his family's home, looked up and remarked, squinting his eyes, "That family's son's wife will come from far away." Jackie's mother heard this and eagerly pressed the fortune teller for details. Like many fortune tellers, this one made a rather vague reply. "She will come from the East," the fortune teller said simply. The geographical designation he had used was just that, "东方" (*dongfang*) or East. I have to grin when I think that I as a Westerner did indeed come to Yang County from the East—namely from Beijing.

Jackie and his father are dog enthusiasts; before Jackie met me, his father wanted to match him up with a local woman who ran a pet store (luckily for me, Jackie didn't agree). After he was once about to return to Beijing and me after visiting his parents by himself, Jackie bought a huge stuffed animal dog, a bulldog. His mother said, "Can't you get Tammy a dog with a prettier face?" But Jackie was impressed by the huge tawny stuffed animal bulldog and insisted on bringing it back to Beijing instead of buying a stuffed animal poodle, which his mother considered cuter. The stuffed animal bulldog we have named JackieTammy is now lounging in our hutong house, wearing long, striped stockings.

At some point, Jackie sent me photos of puppies snuggling in a box via WeChat and looked at me in a meaningful way upon returning home, hoping we could adopt one. I completely understood his desire for something warm and cuddly in the home (me excepted, of course). But keeping pets can be costly and requires a lot of time, so we agreed not to get a pet at that point. But one balmy day in September 2022, as Jackie and I were taking a walk next to the canal near our home, *yuanfen* struck yet again when we spotted a tiny black fur ball wandering aimlessly across a boardwalk, with a drooping, mouse-like tail. We came closer.

"Why, it's a little black cat!" I said, immediately crouching down next to it. Jackie and I didn't speak a lot as we were too busy taking in the sight: It was a tiny black kitten, very thin, and with pus-covered eyes. It was dangerously close to the water, and we weren't sure how it had made it on to the boardwalk. I looked around: There was no sign of a mother cat nearby; after all, you don't want to separate a mother cat from her kittens.

I instinctively scooped up the little black bundle in my arms. It was too late — I was charmed! I knew I wanted to take the kitten home with us. This time I looked at Jackie with pleading eyes; he understood and followed my lead. Without much further ado, we took the kitten to a vet.

Our vet was a very dedicated young woman. "You have a little boy," she said gently, after deftly inspecting the kitten with her gloved hands. She believed the kitten had been abandoned by its mother because it was too weak and had been alone for several days.

"How did it survive by itself?" Jackie asked.

"He probably rummaged through trash," the vet replied. She ran different kinds of tests on the kitten and concluded that he had parasites in his stomach and an eye infection. He also needed nutrients as he wasn't fully weaned at thirty days and his body temperature was too low, so he needed to be kept extra warm. Over the next couple of days, we brought the kitten in for several IV treatments, and he started to gain strength and grow into a handsome, sable-colored Halloween cat with luminous, topaz-yellow eyes who now rules the hutong house roost. We called him "Little Prince," or "Lil P." Of course, he got an equivalent Chinese name as well, 小王子.

I feel blessed every day not only to have the company of my

HUTONG HEARTTHROBS

Big Prince, Jackie, but Little Prince as well. Sometimes Jackie and I had some differences on how to raise our kitten, with Jackie insisting we wipe his tush and paws every time he uses the litter box and accusing me of not spoiling the cat enough. "You're being stingy, you should also be feeding him a bit of home-cooked food," Jackie reprimanded me, pushing a tiny piece of pork chop or beef towards Lil P. Yet Jackie mostly eschews litter box duty and it is mostly I who does the dirty work. Moreover, when I reprimanded Lil P for misbehaving by using the German word for "No!" (*Nein*), Jackie reminded me, "Little Prince is a Chinese cat; he doesn't understand German!"

Several months later, Jackie found another tiny black kitten in a park and brought her to me in a black plastic bag. We called her "Little Princess" and she was with us for a week. She died because she was very small and ill with feline coronavirus; we tried every means possible to save her. We were heartbroken. At the vet's we were able to organize a Buddhist-style "pet farewell service" and cremation for the kitten, which was captured on video, and her remains were given to us in a decorative urn, accompanied by a little poem.

Then we found our "beautiful little dude," rescue cat Hearty, a tuxedo cat like Little Princess had been. Tiny Hearty (心心) was found by a caring garbage collector while he was navigating the streets and given to Polly, a devoted Ukrainian woman who rescues stray animals in Beijing, rehabilitates them and then finds homes for them. Now a third rescue cat, a calico who looks like a Lucky Cat, has joined the ranks; Baby Fortune or 招财 has a raspy meow, and the black rings around her eyes make her look like she is wearing mascara.

Jackie came to the conclusion that many Westerners regard their pets as treasured family members, not mere pets or working animals according to the traditional Chinese view. When he informed his parents of Little Prince as a new addition to the family, his father's first question was, "Do you have mice at home?" This was a legitimate question in the countryside.

Jackie can fly high and let his inner child show, and is very much a creative and imaginative person, enjoying a cool look and a variety of clothes and accessories in part due to his acting vocation. His twin sister Liu Zhi (刘智) appears just the opposite: easy to satisfy in all respects, very much grounded in reality, no-drama, rational and pragmatic. And whereas Jackie can be warm, outgoing and energetic, like their mother, his sister appears more laid back and reserved, like their father.

For example, when Liu Zhi was visiting us in the hutong house for one month, Jackie was in a tizzy because he was looking for a blue T-shirt one morning. Meanwhile, Liu Zhi had brought only two shirts for her stay, the one she was wearing on her back and a spare; she washed and wore the two shirts in turn.

"Here it is, Jackie!" I said, triumphantly holding up one of his blue shirts.

"Not that one," Jackie said.

"This one?" his sister asked, holding up another blue shirt.

"No, not that one... I need my *blue* shirt!"

And it went on like this for a while as we helped Jackie rummage through his big pile of clothes on the sofa. Jackie's extensive wardrobe includes multiple shirts, one with an image of Jackie Chan on it and the slogan "I know Jackie," a periwinkle-colored shirt with Britney Spears on it, although Jackie had no clue who she was, suits, military costumes, clothes with sequins and in fabulous colors and outlandish designs as well as all kinds of sneakers, dress shoes, boots. You name it, Jackie probably has it in his eclectic fashion collection.

Most recently, he bought himself a rainbow-colored suit with a head-turning traditional Dongbei flower pattern (东北大花) on it which looked like a pair of pajamas and a matching one for me. I was normally okay with his fashion choices, but the Dongbei "flower power suits" were too avant-garde and chinoiserie overkill even for me despite them being very fashionable in 2024, perhaps thanks to Douyin influencers. When a security guard at the Ditan Park Temple Fair spotted Jackie in his outfit during the Chinese New Year, he did a double take and said approvingly, "That really gives off Spring Festival vibes."

But I gradually warmed up to the Skittles-colored outfits, paired with Jackie's blond hair, which he had dyed on the occasion of the Lunar New Year and made him look like a K-pop star. (I hope he won't go for Smurf-blue or green hair in the future, although Jackie has been toying with the idea.) You can see us in the Dongbei "flower power outfits" and Jackie as a blond in the photo for this chapter. But back to our quest for Jackie's shirt.

We finally found the "right" blue shirt.

"Jackie, you are lucky," I quipped. "You have two ladies-in-waiting at your service this morning!"

Liu Zhi, a no-nonsense woman, just rolled her eyes at this.

The twins, having very different personalities, sometimes engage in sibling rivalry. They also don't resemble one another very much. Jackie is taller and has a fairer complexion, and they have different features. As children, Liu Zhi appeared very self-assured and independent, whereas Jackie was shy and cried a lot, especially when he missed his sister, Jackie told me.

But that made it all the more entertaining, and Jackie's parents truly stood out in Yang County because of their 龙凤胎 (*longfengtai*, literally meaning "dragon-phoenix twins," or a set of twins of mixed gender) while China still had a one-child policy, officially. In traditional Chinese style, more funds were allocated to the education of the son than the daughter, and preference overall was given to the male child over the female one, a practice still common in China's rural population where money is tight. But Liu Zhi made up for this with her smarts, goal-oriented attitude and hard work. She is now a wedding planner in Hanzhong, not far from their parents' home, and business is brisk.

Meanwhile, Jackie's parents were building an apartment building on their land, which has now been completed, and Jackie spent several weeks there to lend a hand while I was back in the US visiting my mother in the autumn of 2019. He got up early in the morning when the cocks were crowing to help his father, and we would chat before he went out. While we were doing a WeChat video chat with Jackie—he in his hometown and I in Washington, D.C.,—he swung his camera so I could see the construction work in progress. I was intrigued by the rapid progress and two wrought-iron birds, which Jackie said represented both of us, on the gable of the building. And I was shocked to see Jackie's mother, a small and slender woman in her sixties, wearing a construction hat and also lugging bricks together with her son and elderly husband. In China, the "do it yourself" approach clearly applies to many areas. The plan was to have apartments set aside for the family including one for Jackie and myself, with the other apartments being rented out to individuals and businesses for income.

Before construction on the apartment building of Jackie's family was completed, Jackie and I stayed in a hotel when we came to visit, as the apartment his parents were renting was not so suitable for visitors, and of course, as a foreigner I had to register at the local police station. Hotels that accept foreigners usually do that for you automatically, which is more convenient than if you stay at a Chinese individual's home, where you are expected to register by yourself. But on one trip, Jackie and I were unexpectedly asked by our hotel to make the trip to the local police station ourselves.

At the station, a stern-looking policewoman asked me, "Do your parents know you are visiting him?" (nod to Jackie). "Do they approve?" She could clearly see from my passport and appearance that I was legally an adult, and had been for quite some time. When I replied my mother was 75, my father deceased, and that she could see from my passport that I was of age, she seemed satisfied.

Upon checking into the hotel, we raised some eyebrows because we were sharing a room as an unmarried couple, which reminded me of America several decades ago. I am not sure how they knew Jackie and I were unmarried; it might have come up during small talk Jackie engaged in with the receptionist; after all, marital status is not a prerequisite for a couple checking into a hotel room in China. In big Chinese cities, unmarried couples sharing a hotel room is a frequent scenario, but the countryside is more traditional.

This occurred at the Oscar Hotel in Yang County; one would think that its lofty name, a nod to the glitzy Hollywood movie awards, would promise a more worldly approach to tourism. However, we enjoyed the movie theme of the decor—there were a lot of framed photos of mainly Asian but also some Western movie stars as well as film posters, e.g., from *Titanic*. Even American actress Jennifer Aniston, with her girl-next-door charm, smiled at us from her frame.

As Chinese men and foreign women couples are still relatively rare in China, Jackie has been mistaken for my tour guide, and even my translator or Chinese teacher on our trips, which has greatly amused us. In fact, he has been all three to me. When I jokingly asked Jackie what the greatest role he has played so far was, he immediately replied, laughing, "Your leading man" (in China, a leading man in a movie or TV series is called "男一号" or *nan yi hao*, which literally means "number-one man").

Yes, Jackie and I understood each other! We have what in China is called 默契 (*moqi*), which means a mutual, tacit understanding. Often, we have a shared sense of humor. On one occasion, I told Jackie that he was "made in China," and he grinned and gave me a playful slap on the behind.

On other occasions, however, it is hard to communicate humor across the cultural divide because of the language barrier and different ideas about what constitutes humor; it is my impression that many Chinese prefer slapstick to dark humor. When I am in a Chinese movie theater, for instance, watching a comedy, the audience sometimes tends to laugh at different things than I do. But like Jackie, I do occasionally enjoy slapstick, which effortlessly crosses the cultural divide since it does not rely on language or cultural context.

What's more, Jackie's imagination responds well to mine; for example, he calls our rented, snug two-room hutong house a "villa," and the convenient shared bikes, ubiquitous in Beijing that he uses to pick me up after working the night shift "BMWs." This reminds me of a woman featured on the dating show *If You Are the One* (非诚勿扰) who famously said that she "would rather cry in a BMW than laugh on a bicycle" and thus sparked a lot of discussion in China about whether or not money can buy love.

The reactions to our cross-cultural and interracial relationship have varied greatly among the Chinese: incredulity, indifference, disdain, resentment, envy, approval, amusement, curiosity and appreciation. For example, one of Jackie's relatives didn't believe Jackie when he told him he had an American girlfriend. I suppose I was somewhat like Bigfoot or the Loch Ness Monster until I physically showed up in Jackie's hometown. People tend to stare at us unabashedly when we are together, even in such relatively cosmopolitan cities as Beijing, and some smile good-naturedly, especially women. One young Chinese woman said in Chinese, "I wish you well!" when she saw Jackie and me happy together (in front of a KFC, no less).

An acquaintance of Jackie's who worked in a photo shop in Beijing, when meeting me for the first time, saw Jackie helping me into my coat as a male customer walked in, who also witnessed this scene. She and the male customer smiled warmly at each other; I think it was a subtle nod of approval towards Jackie's sweet and chivalrous act and our relationship.

What's more, a young Chinese man went so far as to call Jackie a "hero" for having a foreign girlfriend, a 洋娃娃 (*yang wawa* means "foreign doll," as Jackie has endearingly called me from time to time). I am not sure why the young man was so encouraging. Was it because some Chinese see me partly as their "own" due to my ties to a local man? Meanwhile, from what I could glean from comments on social media, others see getting a foreign girlfriend as a practical and not necessarily inferior solution to helping reduce the rather large number of single Chinese men currently available.

Another, frequent positive reaction we have received is the comment, "You and your significant other have similar features!" This is surprising as Jackie and I are obviously from two different races, but many Chinese believe that common facial traits show a predestination that two people are meant to be together.

One young woman in Jackie's hometown very frankly asked Jackie whether foreigners and Chinese are intimate in the same way. Jackie felt rather abashed and did not wish to answer this very personal question; he wouldn't kiss and tell! I found that occasional shyness and elusiveness of his strangely attractive; maybe it was my hunter instinct. After all, in China, intimacy is not as openly discussed as in some Western countries. What's more, it isn't customary in China to say "I love you" to one's significant other, at least not among older generations. When I have often expressed this sentiment to Jackie, he was surprised at this but happy to reciprocate, adding that Chinese aren't in the habit of doing so (except maybe in TV series). Instead, you let your actions speak for themselves.

But not everyone is pleased by our relationship. Especially among some young Chinese men (singles?) we have encountered a bit of hostility, which might have been rooted in envy. One of Jackie's WeChat contacts was so outraged by Jackie's posting photos of himself and me that he found a way to have Jackie's WeChat account shut down. Someone else called me an "old eagle" preying on a "young chicken" (Jackie, four years younger) on social media, which I actually found quite amusing. When it's an older man with a younger woman, no matter in which country, usually no one bats an eye, but when it comes to women who are with men who are younger, society's double standards are suddenly exposed.

Another young man, whom I knew to be single, appeared to be annoyed by the "lovey-dovey" relationship Jackie and I enjoy. He asked Jackie and me impatiently when we were getting married, as if marriage were a romance-killer, and seated us at an isolated table during an event we were attending that he had helped organize. Yet another disgruntled young Chinese bachelor called our interactions "very corny."

So in order not to cause discomfort or trouble, Jackie suggested we don't hold hands in certain situations, especially in the countryside, which is more traditional and less open to the world.

Indeed, Jackie seems to have more street smarts than I do, although we both grew up in relatively sheltered environments, well protected by our parents. I assume that is because of the rather wild adventures and situations Jackie has experienced as an itinerant worker. I would ultimately come to the conclusion that many Chinese have street smarts, which they need in order to survive in the complicated Chinese society.

A question Jackie and I get asked frequently is how do we communicate? The answer is we speak simple Chinese. A friend of Jackie's has observed that we foreigners are all "children" in China. This is true; occasionally I feel like a child that Jackie is raising in the Chinese culture, while to me, he is a child I try to raise in the Western culture. We are not only the best of friends and lovers to each other, but also occasionally "parent" each other.

I once asked Jackie whether he would speak to me in the same way if I were Chinese, and he said definitely no, because he would be speaking faster and using more complex language including 成语 (*chengyu* or proverbs), because you can express more in a succinct way by using a four-character *chengyu*, which alludes to a story or consists of a historical quotation. "How's your Chinese?" Jackie will tease me when I make a glaring language mistake or fail to understand something he expected me to know after he had taught me.

Jackie said he wants to help me with my Chinese first, and then later we would continue to work harder on his English, although I have been occasionally trying to teach him more English words and phrases. When he went to Sydney to work on a Jackie Chan movie with a stopover in Manila, his first time abroad, I was nervous about him boarding his connecting flight.

I made a bilingual cardboard sign for him with the most important sentences in English he could show to airport staff or fellow passengers to ensure he could smoothly handle any problems. I was relieved when he finally arrived safely. A real extrovert at times, Jackie quickly made some local Chinese friends in Sydney who spoke English and helped him explore the city on his days off.

I have tried to teach Jackie some English words, which I wrote for him in a little black notebook, as a supplement to the knowledge he has gleaned from the immensely popular "Crazy English" courses he had taken before he met me. Here are some examples of our language sessions, with the conversation taking place in Chinese with the exception of the English words.

JACKIE (reclining on the bed): What's the English word for *panda*?
TAMMY (next to him, pulling out the black notebook): "Panda."
JACKIE: "Paper"?
TAMMY: No, "panda."
JACKIE: "Paper"?

Some words are easier than others for Jackie to pronounce; for example, he likes the word *agree*.

TAMMY: I want to spend every day with you!
JACKIE (with a winning smile and speaking English with a bit of an accent), "Agree!"

As some English words are hard for Jackie to pronounce, sometimes a shortcut is called for. Here is another example from when we were celebrating Jackie's birthday in a Shaanxi noodle restaurant; Chinese are in the habit of eating long noodles on their birthday because they symbolize long life. This conversation revolved around the English word *frog*.

JACKIE (picking up a frog-shaped windup toy on the restaurant table): How do you say *frog* in English?
TAMMY: "Frog."
JACKIE: "F---"? (Here, Jackie uttered the famous four-letter word, retaining the most innocent facial expression.)
TAMMY (almost choking on her noodles): No, that's a bad word! Where did you learn that word?!
JACKIE: I've heard that word a lot when watching Hollywood movies. What does it mean?
TAMMY: Just remember the word *toad*.

Now a frog obviously isn't exactly the same as a toad, but for our purposes, it was close enough. Sometimes you just have to be pragmatic when learning a language and discard lofty ideals.

"Did you know Chinese before coming to China?" and "How did you study it?" are questions I get asked frequently. Some foreigners get by living for decades in China without learning any Chinese, for whatever reasons, without any sense of shame, yet I did not wish to remain perpetually ignorant of my surroundings. Learning some Chinese can serve any foreigner very well in China. Indeed, learning a language is no small miracle and no small feat. Language brings people together; it builds bridges. My journey to learn Chinese is a continuous one. It is a winding road fraught with steep hills that often finds me pausing, gasping for breath.

When I first came to China, I shuddered at the thought of being illiterate, which for me was associated with utter helplessness and a lack of self-empowerment. I remember for some reason feeling especially frustrated that I couldn't read the advertisements in the subway station.

I admit my journey might have been smoother if I had studied Chinese systematically at a university perhaps, yet my study of the language was a lot more organic—"patchwork Chinese," as I call it. I only started studying it around the time when I first came to Beijing in 2009. My study efforts involved two basic courses at a language-learning institute that catered to working professionals as well as private tutors and a handful of Chinese language exchange partners. Not to mention some stop-and-go self-study involving books, CDs and many trial-and-error interactions with the Chinese people, which might have stripped me of my self-confidence if I hadn't had a die-hard attitude. And of course, finally there was Jackie, now the leading force in my Chinese studies and my primary private tutor.

All the conventional language-learning methods are to some extent effective if you use them consistently, and if you are more advanced, watching movies is really helpful. Before I had Jackie, in my spare time, I was practicing my Chinese on neighbors and even the security guards who went from shy to gallantly holding the doors open for me. It was around this time that I learned that the Chinese greeting "Have you eaten?" ("你吃饭了吗?") was an idiom and meant nothing more than the superficial American expression "How are you?"

One Chinese friend once told me rather diplomatically, "Tammy, your Chinese is fairly good," and others have made similar comments. But deep down, I know it is far from "fairly good." Chinese people are usually very encouraging to foreigners who make even the slightest attempt at Chinese. Occasional setbacks in communication have prompted me to feel I should shelve my Chinese studies, but sheer necessity and constant encouragement from Jackie have helped refuel my motivation. And so, my language-learning journey continues and probably will continue until my dying day.

10

BADLY BITTEN BY THE ACTING BUG

Jackie has climbed up some rungs on the acting ladder, from playing unpaid to minimally paid extras (a low: corpses) to actual paid, decent roles with some lines. He has played a journalist, a restaurant or bar customer, a soldier, a white-collar worker, a doctor, a policeman, a father, a leasing agent and strangely, even an ancient Egyptian in a commercial for socks. The list goes on. And of course, he has worked as a stand-in in several Jackie Chan movies and is mentioned as such in the closing credits (more on that later).

TAMMY TREICHEL

On one of his resumes, Jackie divided his roles into *wu* (武) and *wen* (文), denoting martial arts and non-martial arts roles, respectively. An example of a "wu" role would be a soldier, whereas a white-collar worker would be a "wen" role. Actors also hang up their resumes in copy shops near the hotels frequented by casting directors in the hopes that they would catch their eye.

I have accompanied Jackie to these hotels numerous times. Casting directors rented rooms in mostly shabby, cigarette smoke-filled rooms for extended periods of time, where they both slept and worked. In the hotel lobby, there were posters on a pin board featuring the movie titles and roles and the room number of the casting director. After determining which movies you were interested in, you went to the designated hotel rooms and knocked on the doors, cold turkey. If no one opened the door, Jackie would push his resume under the door if he was seriously interested in a certain role. If the door was opened, you engaged in mostly polite chit-chat with the casting director or an assistant and gave them your resume. Sometimes they would also film a self-introduction video of the auditioning actor.

The rooms were often filled with orderly or disorderly stacks of resumes, either spread on the bed or stacked on a table, with photos of the actors that had already been cast in roles pinned underneath a character's name on a board. When Jackie introduced me to one casting director, he said I was not bad-looking and might be able to do some commercials. That encounter did not lead to a gig, but it was a feel-good experience nonetheless.

Sometimes in the hotel hallways, Jackie and I would bump into actors he had met on previous movie sets, and we would exchange tips on where there might be suitable roles. All kinds of people were looking for roles, children, young adults, the elderly, Chinese and foreigners, all looking for stardom, or at least their fifteen minutes of fame.

Some casting directors were quite polite, but occasionally there were some who were downright rude. Jackie told me a fellow actor had given a casting director his resume, and when the actor turned his back, the casting director tore his resume in two and tossed it in the trash. Jackie distributed his resumes sparingly as they were printed on good paper. Once he didn't have his resume on hand after he had run out of copies, so he had to improvise. But for an actor, improvisation shouldn't be a problem, right? "I am the resume," he told that casting director with a disarming smile and I almost burst out laughing.

"Rocky (a character played by Sylvester Stallone in the eponymous 1976 movie; to Jackie, Rocky has become synonymous with the actor and is one of his favorite inspirational examples) went on five thousand interviews before landing his big break," Jackie reminded me.

Now I don't know whether Stallone really went on five thousand interviews that ended in rejections — in China, people sometimes play fast and loose with numbers — but the point was, Stallone was incredibly persistent.

One evening after a busy afternoon distributing resumes, Jackie suggested I recite the sentence, "I want to be famous" in Chinese over and over again. I laughed out loud; what a crazy idea! "Whatever for?" I asked.

"That's what acting is about, repeating your lines over and over again," Jackie said simply. When ordinary actors aren't shooting, they read newspapers or texts in other formats out loud to practice their pronunciation, hit the gym to stay in shape, groom themselves (like having their hair and nails done), work odd jobs to tide themselves over financially, and of course look for their next gig, he said.

I spent so much time hearing about Jackie's determination to get a role, going with him to distribute resumes, hearing about his adventures, vicariously experiencing his exhilaration and his downers that the world of acting, in a way, became my world, too. And being a woman of adventure, I wondered if I could have a little piece of it.

Jackie coached me, saying that if I ever landed a gig, I should remember not to blink while the camera was rolling, and when delivering my lines, look at my fellow actor directly, just above the forehead, but not into my fellow actor's eyes as that might make you or the other person nervous. As for the lines, "Remember them with your mouth, not just your mind," he advised me.

I sent out resumes looking for possible roles for foreign women. One casting director was looking for a foreigner to play a female villain. He looked me up and down and immediately dismissed me. Another application for a gangster role didn't get any response. There are fewer roles, especially demanding ones, for foreign women than there are for foreign men, but there are some if you look carefully and stay alert.

For example, Jackie and I ran into a casting director called Rex at a hotel. Rex took an interest in me for playing an American researcher called "Babala" in a TV series. "What a strange name!" I thought. "Why do Rex and Jackie always refer to this character as 'Babala'?" Then it occurred to me that they were actually pronouncing the English word "Barbara" in the Chinese way (the /r/ and /l/ sounds in English are hard to distinguish for many Chinese). Now "Barbara" means "foreigner" in ancient Greek, which as you will see was a very suitable name in this TV series' context.

Rex spoke English pretty well and told me more about the plot and the character I was supposed to play. As I would find out, such details were often not divulged before the filming actually started; an actor was left to his or her own devices, do his or her own research into historical characters, or bring his or her own creativity into "shaping" a character if it was a fictional one and see if the director liked one's rendition.

Barbara was the American wife of a Chinese man who had married her for a US green card, and she had a cute little son with a baby face from a previous marriage, Rex told me. She would wear outdoor gear and glasses, as she was conducting research in one of China's remote provinces, and was of a serious, bookish disposition. Barbara would visit her new in-laws in China for the first time and would speak some lines in English and some very simple Chinese. That role sounded like a good fit for me, but there was one catch.

When Rex mentioned they would put Barbara in blue jeans, Jackie objected. "But Tammy doesn't like to wear jeans!" he exclaimed. I then thought, "Oh no, I hope that remark won't diminish my chances of making my acting debut in China." But Jackie's comment did not deter Rex.

"Show surprise and forget your previous experiences and acclimatization to China," Rex suggested. "Imagine you are coming to China for the first time!"

When he asked me whether I had any more questions, I said yes. Although the role of Barbara was obviously a modest one, and far less developed than the roles of the main characters, I wanted to know more about what the producers had in mind. I am always interested in what motivates people to do certain things and of course wanted to do an excellent job.

"Is it a gradual process for Barbara to realize her Chinese husband had married her for a green card, or is it a sudden realization, or does she know all along or is she completely in the dark as regards her husband's motive?"

"That's a good question," Rex replied. "I haven't given it a lot of thought. But I believe that the two possibly do have some feelings for each other." Although this did not directly answer my question, I liked the fact that there was apparently some complexity involved. After all, even a relationship that might be primarily utilitarian did not necessarily have to lack warmth.

Shooting would take place in Tianjin. Rex and his crew took several photos of me propping up my chin with my hand and we would later have some back and forth regarding shooting dates and other details. But then Rex suddenly left the film crew and I was not contacted about the role again. Perhaps the role had been written out of the script or they had found someone else? Things changing suddenly was a frequent scenario in the acting industry; you got cast or lost a role in the blink of an eye, even after filming had started, and sometimes on a whim. But that I had been considered for a film role at all encouraged me to continue to pursue my new acting hobby under Jackie's tutelage.

As I write, security has been tightened in the hotels where actors solicit casting directors and hand out resumes, because some actors and actresses have been taken advantage of by the casting directors, for example by paying up front for a role—actors should never pay for a role but be paid instead. And for women there were casting couches, which occurs everywhere. So for the sake of safety and convenience, today a lot of roles are advertised online or even more frequently, on WeChat.

I found my first real role online, and it would be the "role of a lifetime" or at least the highlight of my acting hobby to date. A film studio was looking for someone to play the role of Joan Hinton, an American nuclear physicist who had chosen China over the atom bomb, for a short film. The studio needed someone who resembled her to a certain extent, could speak some Chinese, accent notwithstanding, and ride a horse. It was a dream role for me: I could play a real-life historical character and an intelligent woman who had contributed to China's development and had a certain amount of depth, not a dumb stock character.

The nightmare of some actors who take their calling seriously is being typecast; this was only a hobby for me, but I still hoped that I wouldn't be in that situation. One man had told me rather dismissively that I could only play mom or teacher types because of my looks and age, but it turned out that I would find a niche playing intellectual characters.

For example, I would go on to play a French writer called Jeanne for a Chinese movie, and although the director initially had a real Frenchwoman who looked like Juliette Binoche in mind for the role, he ultimately ended up with me because he couldn't go to France to film due to Covid-19. That was an unexpected stroke of luck. When the director saw me, he exclaimed rather excitedly, "You look exactly like a writer!" Interestingly, as Jeanne, I played opposite a young Russian woman who looked like a blond bombshell and usually played the sexy, cold-blooded killer type, but this time was cast as a wholesome mom to a cherubic-looking little boy.

So how did I land my first acting gig, playing Joan Hinton?

Somewhat on a whim, I applied to an opening for two foreign actors, an American expat couple who "are going to visit their friend Gala in Inner Mongolia." Despite my lack of acting experience, the casting director still showed interest in me after viewing my materials, and after some back and forth via an agent, and a makeup and audition session, I was given the part and four days to prepare. I suspect it was my haircut, a bob, as well as a rough physical resemblance despite our large age difference of over two decades that landed me the role of a sixty-plus-year-old Joan Hinton.

Hinton (1921-2010) was born in Chicago and was one of the few women nuclear physicists who participated in America's Manhattan Project to build an atom bomb during World War

II. Being a sort of daredevil, she snuck away on a motorcycle to witness the Trinity Test. Greatly disillusioned after bombs were actually dropped on Hiroshima and Nagasaki, Hinton went to China in 1948. In China's Yan'an, she married Erwin Engst, a cattle expert. They had three children together. Hinton became a devoted follower of the communist cause. During the McCarthy era of the 1950s, she was depicted as a "blond traitor" and trench-coated femme fatale, and more sensationally, as a Cold War Mata Hari in the US, labels that she laughed off.

Hinton used her science background to help design automated milking and pasteurizing machines as well as other farming equipment in China to help build a socialist economy. In fact, she was quoted as saying that she did not want to use her talents to kill people but help them enjoy a better life instead. No matter what the historic developments in China, she remained committed to the cause. After her husband's death in 2003, she spent her remaining days on a farm near Beijing, taking care of her 200 cows.

I would discover from old footage dating back to about 1985 after which our film was to be modeled that Hinton's character and mine appeared to be poles apart—she came across as very natural, earthy, warm-hearted and peppy, whereas I am more reserved and quiet and move more slowly. Ideologically, we are also complete opposites. When she laughed, she showed her teeth, whereas I rarely laugh, and when I smile, I keep my lips closed.

Michael Crook, who is exceptionally knowledgeable about China's old "foreign friends," called Hinton a "firebrand" who liked to play the violin. According to the *China Daily*, she owned a 19th-century Italian violin, her most prized possession. Also, Hinton had a more athletic build than I do—after all, "atomic Joan" had at one point qualified as an Olympic skier.

HUTONG HEARTTHROBS

I prepared for the role after work at home by learning more about Hinton — she garnered my great respect when I discovered she had earned a PhD in physics — singing aloud the lyrics for the banquet scene, and practicing the greeting and farewell scenes with Jackie, with Jackie's smart phone filming me to see how I looked like on camera.

The short film had four scenes, all set in Erdos, Inner Mongolia. In the first scene, Hinton and her husband dismount from their horses, and greet Gala and their other Inner Mongolian friends with bear hugs and handshakes. In the second, the couple is given a welcome banquet by their Inner Mongolian hosts on the grasslands. In the third, Gala hosts them for a meal in her home. In the final scene, the couple bid an emotional farewell to Gala and the other Inner Mongolians.

Jackie and I would stay in Erdos for three days. We landed in Yinchuan, Ningxia province, and took a 4x4 for about two hours to Erdos. Traveling with us was a fairly young half-British, half-Swedish actor who would play my husband. The actor had strawberry-blond hair and pale blue eyes. It turned out he was an experienced actor called Adam who had played various roles for TV series, such as a member of the Flying Tigers or a German spy. Adam was dressed in a black jumpsuit, the only other foreigner in view except for myself, and had a self-assured aura.

As we crossed the border into Inner Mongolia, we saw poplar trees, sheep dotting the grasslands, a tiny public bus and a sand desert in the distance before arriving in Erdos. In the evening we were taken to a multi-story building not far away from our hotel, where I caught my first glimpse of Gala — the actress who would play Hinton's close Inner Mongolian friend — wearing a sky-blue robe. The actress looked exactly like the original Gala in the documentary. Our Gala turned out to be a feisty woman with a bit of a temper, and I felt we forged a bond from the very beginning.

The evening was devoted to becoming acquainted with our fellow actors and building the chemistry needed to make a good movie—Adam, Gala and an Inner Mongolian dancing troupe as well as musicians were all present. The Inner Mongolians were dressed in their traditional costumes and headdresses as well as embroidered boots, which they nowadays only wear on special occasions. They were a very welcoming and hospitable bunch, and we had lots of fun practicing our scenes with props—for example, substituting a plastic bottle for liquor and a small suitcase for a platter with mutton.

We foreign actors also learned a bit about Inner Mongolian culture. Mongolians like to drink *kumis*, which is fermented mare's milk—and when my fellow foreign actor Adam referred to the blue ceremonial scarf used by Mongolians by uttering the Chinese word for "scarf," the director corrected him by saying it was actually called a *hada*, a term also used for scarves in Tibetan culture.

Adam and I had to get up early the next morning for a long makeup session. In the hotel, I heard him practicing his Chinese song "Shanbei is a good place" in the shower next door while I was slipping into my costume—a white blouse, blue jacket with a ballpoint pen stuck in the front pocket, blue overalls and ochre-colored "liberation shoes" that pinched my size-41 feet—a typical outfit worn by Chinese people in the Mao era. One local would later ask me whether Americans also dressed that way, but everyone else immediately recognized the period costume.

In the darkness of the night, we drove to a private home belonging to a local family that would double as our base for makeup sessions and costume changes, an Oriental "little house on the prairie," as Adam called it, complete with a water pump and an outhouse.

HUTONG HEARTTHROBS

Within two hours, the makeup artists' professional skills had transformed us into sexagenarians, with Adam wearing a bald cap with tufts of hair glued to the back and me wearing a mop-like gray wig with strands of my natural hair that had been colored with a gray paint pen sticking out. We were asked not to lie down for a nap, despite being in sore need of one, in order not to ruin our makeup and hair.

It was in a building at the back of the house that we filmed the third scene in Gala's home. We had to sit cross-legged on a heatable brick bed called a *kang* (炕), Inner Mongolian-style. In front of us were two narrow tables with snacks, spirits and a real pack of cigarettes. My film husband would have to light several cigarettes for Gala, who got to smoke some before we wrapped up the scene.

It was during this scene that Hinton and her husband had to perform their singing numbers in Chinese behind a smoke screen. My lyrics in Chinese were: "I am brave and nothing I fear... throw a bomb down, I say it's a watermelon!" My delivery was met with gusto and applause from the Inner Mongolians every time, despite the fact that I was a horrible singer. I gave my best performance after accidentally being given a cup of Chinese 白酒 (*baijiu*, or spirits) by Adam, who thought it was water.

We got up around 3:00 a.m. the next day; I only got roughly three hours of sleep. Some of us were a bit grouchy when we arrived at our base, and I noticed that the actress playing Gala had bloodshot eyes and her braids were hanging down limply. Again, lying on the couch was not an option because of our elaborate makeup and hairdos, so we walked around in a stupor before breakfast was served.

That day we would shoot Scene 1, during which Hinton and her husband ride towards their Inner Mongolian friends and greet each other with great excitement. Although I had only ridden for tourism purposes before, the riding scene went down well for me because Jackie had given me several last-minute instructions on how to ride a horse. Still, I needed to strike a balance between being mindful of safety (we weren't wearing helmets as the real Hinton and her husband hadn't worn any either) and ensuring my wig stayed in place.

Another challenge was the temperament of my horse, a gelding, which was exceptionally stubborn and liked to graze, so I had to use a lot of force to egg him on. Once we had to do the scene over again because my horse wouldn't budge, while Adam's had already galloped over to Gala and the rest of our Inner Mongolian welcoming committee. Our Inner Mongolian co-stars sighed loudly and made exasperated noises at my delay, and I returned to the starting point with my tail between my legs; meanwhile, my little horse couldn't care less and was just interested in filling his belly.

Another take had me dismounting rather slowly, as befitted a senior Hinton, while Adam — who liked to show off his good riding skills — had already dismounted and was swiftly moving towards our friends. A local exclaimed, "A sixty-plus-year-old man can't possibly dismount so fast!"

A real treat while shooting that scene was watching some Inner Mongolians galloping across the grasslands with such natural grace and ease — it seemed that the locals could work their horses as Americans their cars.

The next scene to be shot was Scene 2, where Hinton and her husband are given a welcome banquet (note: in movies and TV series, scenes are rarely shot in sequence). Our Inner Mongolian hosts surrounded us in a circle while Adam and I were sitting on the ground, cross-legged, in front of a low table containing a real dismembered lamb. The scene called for me to engage in a wrestling match with Gala, with no one emerging as the clear winner. While the camera was rolling during one take, I got so excited about the wrestling that I accidentally defeated Gala. After the director yelled "咔!" ("*ka*" or "cut"), some Inner Mongolians burst out laughing and gave me a thumbs-up, and I apologized profusely to the actress who was playing Gala; she was looking quite displeased. I was determined to get the wrestling scene right as we had to wrap up filming by evening and then return to the airport.

In the late afternoon, we had to redo the farewell scene between Gala and Hinton, as the director felt that the actress playing Gala had come across as too awkward while we were filming the scene the day before. The director wanted a more emotional Gala—after all, who knew whether Hinton and Gala would ever meet again? So without further ado, Gala was given eye drops and asked to think of something sad, which got the tears flowing. We had to do about ten takes for this scene over two days, so this was clearly the most difficult scene in our relatively simple film as it's generally easier for an actor to express joy and excitement than grief; although I would later encounter actors who could cry on command. Afterwards, it was a wrap.

What I profoundly enjoyed about this experience was becoming acquainted with the acting world—part of the fun was having to quickly adapt to new situations, people, schedules and tasks while fully tapping my physical and mental reserves. Of course, it was also very insightful to interact with and learn more about the Inner Mongolians, one of China's ethnic minorities. Last but not least, I was intrigued to learn more about Hinton and ask the locals about her.

The husband of one of the Inner Mongolian musicians told me he had met Hinton personally in 1985 or so while working with the police unit in charge of protecting her and her husband as foreigners were scarce in the area. He described her as lively and easygoing. Another local remembered her as being somewhat taller than I am, but he felt her personality was similar to mine as she was cheerful. He also remembered she liked to crack jokes.

I had tried my best to revive Joan Hinton for those who had experienced her and give the film crew and our local hosts the best rendition of this unusual foreigner that I possibly could. It took almost no time to warm up to the Inner Mongolians on set, thanks in part to Jackie's extrovert nature and help in breaking the ice. Just one little local boy cried upon seeing me all messy in my wig and makeup the first day and told his mother he was afraid, but the second day already found him waving to me.

After my stint, I felt a little down, because "Joan" had become a part of me, and Jackie and I had to leave our new colorful Inner Mongolian friends behind and get back to the daily grind in Beijing after all that excitement on the grasslands. It was a very strange and somewhat sad feeling of having to step from a fictitious, somewhat magical world back into the real one, and the transition took about one day for me. I had never experienced such a feeling before. Maybe I had unconsciously engaged in some method acting in trying to prepare for my role and thus had a hard time shaking off my new persona after the fun was over?

I think everyone was satisfied with our performance; when Jackie asked the director how I had performed, he replied that I had done a good job. Jackie himself said he was surprised by my acting debut. But actually, I had to thank Jackie for the successful outcome of this stint — not only did his presence provide me with a lot of moral support, but his guidance both before the filming and on the ground was invaluable.

The film crew kindly let Jackie accompany me to Inner Mongolia, and lodged and fed him as well. He was even given a long blue robe and put in the back of the banquet scene as a half-visible extra because he was wearing sneakers, which the actors weren't supposed to be wearing in the film. (Similarly, Adam was wearing Nike socks, and he needed to be careful when riding that the Nike logo wouldn't show.)

Jackie looked very handsome, with his dark blue robe complementing his raven-black hair, and he would wink at me or give me tips during our breaks. When Adam and I weren't needed for the riding scene, he, Jackie and I took refuge in a jeep because the sun was scorching and the dust was blowing over the grasslands.

Jackie practiced the wrestling scene with me numerous times and as previously mentioned also gave me a crash course on how to ride a horse; he knew how to ride from his previous film stints. I actually knew absolutely nothing about riding a horse, but considered myself an occasional fast learner and a believer in common sense. I wasn't afraid; after all, I had ridden a stout little Inner Mongolian horse with my mother when she had come to visit me in China earlier under the supervision of a guide.

However, Jackie admitted to me afterwards, "I was worried that you could get injured!" But he knew it was futile to dissuade me from accepting the part as I was quite stubborn and strong-willed. I needed to indulge my fantasy and be Joan Hinton, if only for a few short days!

Before we traveled to Inner Mongolia, Jackie mentored me extensively at home, and I was an eager student. "Acting isn't a joke," he said. He then told me that when he was starting out as an actor and playing a soldier, he blinked his eyes once while the camera was rolling and the explosives were going off.

The scene needed to be reshot, which took an extra hour of labor and more explosives (a lot of money in terms of crew members' time and material). The director of course wasn't pleased. "Who hired this knucklehead?!" he stormed. Jackie said he just carried on and maintained a good work attitude and his self-confidence despite the director's outburst. After all, the show must go on.

With Jackie, I practiced singing for my role, as well as how to move faster and more spontaneously, in keeping with Hinton's character as we could ascertain from the old footage we had watched of her. I also tried to learn as much as I could online about her. Jackie and I practiced the greeting and farewell scene numerous times in our hutong house with a kangaroo stuffed animal he had bought when he was filming in Australia. I don't know how many times I shook its paws. We were a far cry from Hollywood, that's for sure, but in life you always need to know how to help yourself.

Adam, who played my husband Erwin Engst, had graduated from either Britain's Oxford or Cambridge University with an arts degree. We got to know Adam a little bit better on the long drive back to the airport in Ningxia, from where we would fly back to Beijing.

"What are you going to do with an arts degree? University sure doesn't teach you many things in life, such as how to earn a living," Adam remarked. He was absolutely right about that. As an experienced actor, Adam appeared to have seen it all and spent his spare time on set wisely catching up on sleep or recharging his batteries for the next scene instead of socializing with the film crew.

He appeared quite reserved and cracked a smile only once, and that was when I was rehearsing my singing; it must have been apparent to Adam and the Inner Mongolians that my musical capabilities were rather limited. After all, this stint didn't require an opera singer. So I too "drew a tiger while using a cat as a model" as Jackie had done before when "playing dead" during one of his acting stints: I did a simple, rather crude imitation of

Hinton singing her tune in the old footage.

Adam said something I was unable to forget: "Actors are like prostitutes. Not only are you paid for your time, you are paid to fulfill your customer's fantasies." I was quite taken aback by this rather explicit simile, but there was definitely something to it. This reminded me of a comment Jackie had previously made that actors are merely commodities. But a certain degree of professionalism is always required, for example next to the actual skills, punctuality and a good work ethic are expected, as is confidentiality before a film is released.

For most actors, however, their work does not make for a comfortable and conventional everyday existence. Being an actor involves a lot of patience, preparation and waiting — waiting for the right role, applying, then an agonizing wait to see whether you are chosen and once you are cast, preparing for your role by memorizing your lines, and maybe doing some research, and perhaps also making some adjustments to your physical appearance such as coloring your hair or getting into a certain shape, and later waiting on set for your scene or scenes to be shot while going over your lines again after you have been put into costume and makeup.

When you are shooting, there could be a lot of blood, sweat and tears involved (literally) and of course, make sure you don't get stage fright and forget your lines, which is a cardinal sin in the acting industry. And once it's a wrap and you are not shooting anymore, you need to work on your various skills and ensure you stay fit and presentable while hunting for your next role.

As opposed to the office jobs I was used to, I discovered you need an enormous amount of mental and physical stamina to be an actor. When shooting, sometimes you can only sleep for a few hours at night, and sometimes you can't go to the restroom for several hours. Many people mistakenly think that acting is full of rainbows and unicorns, but the truth is far less glamorous. Actors who are truly committed to their craft are really willing to "suffer for one's art," as the saying goes.

To some, like Jackie, acting was more than a career, it was a way of life, or a calling. "Acting is life," Jackie told me. But sometimes, and I have to laugh when I think of it, the opposite is true. Jackie on another occasion said that "As long as you know your lines, acting is like playing." My conclusion was: Acting certainly isn't for everyone, only for the hardy in body and mind.

"Shooting a movie is hard work. But if you don't taste bitterness, you can't taste sweetness," Jackie told me, referring to the sweetness of seeing yourself perform on the big screen or your name in the closing credits, or taking pride in simply having put on a stellar performance.

11

False leads, dead ends — and lots of fun!

There are thousands of actors and actresses from different countries and of different stripes and varying skill sets in Beijing alone, all hoping to make it big.

Many ads for acting stints lack basic information such as shooting dates, roles and rates, and often the English (if any) leaves a lot to be desired. Many roles demand that men or women must be young and beautiful or handsome or blond — people in the film industry don't mince words. And sometimes a role is advertised as an acting stint when what is actually wanted is just a pretty face or even a model without any real acting skills.

You can find all kinds of ads for extras, models, hand models, clowns, magicians, musicians, boxers, MCs, KTV or mermaid costume girls to Santa Claus, for any kind of roles from smaller ones to those of leading men and women. Here are some real-life examples of recruitment ads for foreign actors that I found on WeChat:

"Beijing notice: tvc [TV commercial] shooting, duration is 18th-20th, one day of these days! Need 2 white skin European model or actor.

① man age 28-35 years old, look like handsome, rich and same like peers in the elite.

② girl, age 25-30 years old, beautiful and look like experts or peers in the elite!

Above 2 character, if your face ordinary, don't fit character require, don't send your materials, it's waste our time!"

Another ad conveyed a lot of excitement due to the use, or rather overuse, of exclamation points: "Filming! Start on 3.28! Work continuously for 20 days! Mass actors! As long as men! 50 people! Need the following countries: America, Greece, Brazil, Chile, Nigeria, Germany! Or friends like these countries! Require sports foundation! Regular fitness can also! Don't be afraid of suffering! If you can work, please send me actor information and videos, thank you."

This ad was more low-key, but also not very specific: "Shooting on January 10 requires two foreign whites, a man with long hair to play Newton and a man to play Van Gogh, as long as he is in Shanghai."

Another production was looking for a special kind of actor: "Beijing filming on the 25th. We need an obedient, small-sized dog with shooting experience."

And this recruitment ad was posted around Christmas time:

"Hangzhou city, watching for an old fat man dressed like a Santa Claus, from 22th-25th, 3-4 sets per day, 20 mins per set. You need an older male model. You'd better be a little fat. Thank you."

Or simply: "Fat men in Europe and America contact me" and one of my personal favorites: "To make a movie, you need to be about 50 years old."

In the cutthroat search for your next role, recruitment ads such as these provide some much-needed comic relief.

After my stint as Joan Hinton, the next gig I landed was that of a doctor in a commercial. For this stint I was paired up with a professional Russian actor who usually plays gangsters. We were put into white jackets and given goggles. Despite my having large hands to go with my large feet, the one-size-fits-all rubber gloves they gave me were too large, so they were fastened around my wrists with rubber bands; I felt like my blood circulation was being cut off. The film lot in Beijing's suburbs where we were filming featured a fake boxing ring, a replica of a subway car and the reconstructed interior of a plane, as well as a lab-like setting, where our shooting took place.

Although it was very stuffy in the August heat and we were sweating it out in our lab coats, the experience was far less physically demanding than my Hinton act as there were no lines. The director just wanted us to look like doctors and strike doctor-like poses, such as holding up vials, looking through a microscope, consulting around a meeting table, and (for me) holding a clipboard while pretending to hold an erudite discussion with my fellow Russian "doctor" colleague.

I underwent a role reversal in another project by playing a patient in a short film about Traditional Chinese Medicine (TCM). The doctor was played by a middle-aged Tibetan woman from Qinghai province with beautiful doe-shaped eyes and a large aquiline nose who was a TCM doctor in real life in the hospital we were shooting in. I was playing a patient undergoing moxibustion treatment, which involves the burning of mugwort leaves, and had to feign my admiration of the moxa cones, which looked either like animal droppings or chocolate truffles she was burning on my shoulder. However, the smoke repeatedly got into my eyes and made me uncomfortable so we had to repeat the scene multiple times.

This was my second experience with moxibustion; Jackie had once applied this remedy to me when my back muscles were tense. I found the warmth of the moxa cones provided a temporary relief from my strained muscles. TCM is definitely worth exploring.

In January 2018, I played the part of a mother in a short movie called *I'm Spending Spring Festival in China* (我在中国过春节). "Mom" encourages her reluctant daughter to go to China despite the negative media reports and enjoy the Spring Festival there. The Mom character is a stock character and considered suitable for foreign women of my age in China (30-40+ years old). The dialogue was almost exclusively in English.

The film location was a swanky villa, about an hour's drive from downtown Beijing, built in a bizarre interpretation of Western style. Mom was in two out of six scenes. In the first scene, I was preparing breakfast. When filming the scene, I had to multi-task, using kitchen props and chatting at the same time. When I was asked to cut a piece of fruit and say my lines, it didn't look natural, so I tried cutting a stale piece of toast instead but had to be careful not to injure myself with the knife.

The kitchen scene was my least favorite because, let's face it, in real life I am a terrible cook (I leave that to Jackie) and having no children myself, being maternal upon command was a challenge. I tried hard to channel a cross between my own mother and perennially perky Carol Brady from the American

TV series *The Brady Bunch* into the role, doling out maternal advice to her children from behind the kitchen counter. Oh, but I did look the part in an oversized sweater and large plastic, horn-rimmed glasses! "Damn, that's an ugly sweater," my sister Heidi commented after seeing the film later on. "That's my own sweater!" I replied. Looking a bit dowdy fulfilled its purpose of making me look more mature, and I was thus in no danger whatsoever of outdoing my rather cool-looking daughter.

As for the horn-rimmed glasses, Jackie and I had bought them at a clothes market near the Beijing Zoo, originally to be used for my role as Barbara the researcher, and they had made their debut in this little film. On the one hand, they made me look more like a seasoned mom, but on the other, the plastic caused a glare so the kitchen scene needed to be reshot each time the lenses hit the light. This greatly irritated the director, who had a type-A personality. Actors are often asked to bring their own clothes or accessories to the set, saving the production team the trouble of having to take your measurements and providing outfits. If your ensemble doesn't work, there are often backup costumes or improvised solutions.

At the end of the day, I felt I had bonded with my foreign film family on the set over our shared challenges and experiences. That was one reason I so enjoyed my acting stints. Next to gaining a better insight into Jackie's world, I could make both Chinese and foreign friends while at the same time practicing my Mandarin or learning different skills.

Talking about different skills, I made one foray into a subcategory of acting: voice acting. I auditioned to voice a role in an adaptation of Mark Twain's classic *The Adventures of Tom Sawyer*. The "audition" consisted of recording some sentences on my smart phone. I was asked, "Can you read any boy lines? We'd like to have a girl speak as a boy. You can choose any character.

For example, Bart Simpson's voice actor is a female. That's what we are looking for. Can you do that?"

I eventually landed both the parts of Tom Sawyer and his little girlfriend, Amy. Whereas Tom was a bright and naughty 12-year-old boy, Amy was his dream girl who was described as having the upper hand in the relationship and putting on airs.

When I arrived at the recording studio, I was greeted by Justa, a fiery young Polish woman who used fluent Chinese to communicate with the studio staff. I was ushered into a soundproof room with a big microphone, headphones and recording equipment, while Justa, Jackie and the staff were in an adjacent room, separated by a thick pane of glass.

While doing the recording project, I had to be careful not to put my mouth too close to the microphone, nor tap the table and flip the pages of the script as this would mar the recording. Jackie, too, gave me some pointers, reminding me to use "power" when reading my lines. He had also done some voice recordings and remembered he had "blood coming out of his nose and ears" (figuratively, of course) because doing voice work requires a lot of effort and patience. When we took a break, Jackie came to my soundproof room to hand me a candy bar he had tucked away in his jacket.

During the recording, I had to make chewing sounds (they had me eat a pear to achieve this effect), yell, hiss, lisp, do kissing sounds, giggle, laugh, put on airs, be angry, sob—in other words, run the whole gamut of emotions as Tom and Amy. Sometimes, when recording the part of Tom, I slipped back into my original woman's voice and Justa had to remind me to jump back into Tom's character.

When I did Amy's voice, Justa also provided valuable directions. "Remember, you're very proud of your father," Justa directed me at one point (Amy's father was a judge) or, "You really like Tom, and you're excited to be on a date with him" (in a cave nonetheless). "You're a PRINCESS!"

As for Tom, when interacting with Amy, Justa told me to "remember, Amy is your dream girl" and when I wasn't excited enough about offering Amy water to drink on "our" date in a cave, Justa was quick to point it out. "Listen to yourself. Do you sound excited? No, you sound bored!"

Justa was a good "director," nudging me in the right direction to "find my voice," be it Tom's or Amy's. She said I did Amy's voice particularly well; in fact my mother once called me a "drama queen" when I was young and having a hissy fit. But I preferred doing Tom's voice because his adventurous character and the sentences he uttered were more appealing to me; my favorite part was yelling, "Let's become pirates and be free!" to the other little boys, as that line to me expressed all the unfettered joy and adventurousness of childhood.

Another acting stint saw me playing a modern-day hostess for a black tea commercial which we filmed in a Western-style hotel on the outskirts of Beijing. The hotel featured aristocratic European trappings: statues of British "Beefeaters" outside the entrance, chandeliers, fireplaces, a suit of armor, baroque-style paintings and a copy of a famous large portrait of the Empress Elisabeth (Sisi) of Austria in the lobby.

The second actress who had been recruited for the commercial was a bubbly young Ukrainian woman called Katy who would also play a Bond girl in action movies. Her permed blond hair, swept up, perfectly matched the 18th-century style slate gray hoop skirt she was given to wear, while I was put into a yellow qipao. Katy liked to pose with her tea cup and twirl around with it on set, and practiced some quick kung fu moves with Jackie in the bathroom while not shooting.

While sipping tea, I had to "converse" with a Chinese man

sitting on a sofa to my right. The point was showing me chatting with my tea party guests while savoring tea. He was a local artist who specialized in nude photography, and our conversation about his specialty did not last very long as I neither knew anything about nude photography nor was particularly interested in his vocation, although I tried my very best to feign interest and thankfully, this sufficed to keep the tea flowing. Although my Chinese "party guests" and I gradually ran dry of topics and I was quite eager to escape the conversation about nude photography, we never got thirsty thanks to the never-ending tea refills. I truly felt like Alice in Wonderland, seated in my wing chair at a tea party.

The tea commercial was pretty well made, I think "epic" would be the right word for it, as it covered the history of black tea and involved a lot of different actors, all Chinese except for myself, Katy, who played a noblewoman, and a Russian actor who was recruited to play Robert Fortune, the botanist and "tea thief" who smuggled tea plants out of China and took them to British-controlled India on behalf on the British East India Company.

Another gig involved my being recruited to play a middle-aged woman for a TV series called *I'm Waiting for You in Beijing* (often rather strangely translated as *Wait You in Beijing*, 我在北京等你) starring the formerly famous (and now infamous) Chinese actor, singer and teen idol Li Yifeng (李易峰). When I auditioned for the role, I played a woman who was arguing with her lawyer (who would be played by Li Yifeng) about her son's death sentence. While making the audition video, I channeled all my anger over my father's passing and other grievances into the role, things that made me really feel outraged, and then sent the video to the agent. I could see even Jackie was quite impressed by my fury, which as opposed to my occasional annoyance when things aren't going smoothly in China, is never on display at home. "Do you have a white T-shirt?" the agent asked. I was cast immediately.

I would visit the film set twice for this role with Jackie accompanying me. The first time I came, they suddenly changed my role into that of a middle-aged New Yorker woman trying to trick a lawyer (Li Yifeng) into believing she had recognized a lost dog, a Golden Retriever called "Cookie," in order to claim money. Versed in human nature, the lawyer exposes her and she leaves angrily without claiming the reward. I had to prepare the lines *ad hoc* in both English and Chinese, which wasn't that hard as I only had several lines of dialogue.

Although we didn't get around to shooting my scene that day, which is common when making movies or TV series, I did get to see Li Yifeng in person, wearing a knit cobalt blue sweater and jeans. What struck me most about him were his prominent thick eyebrows and aloof air. I saw him either sitting in the studio on a camp chair next to the director or speeding around the film lot on a scooter.

I personally didn't understand what the fuss was about. To me, he was just another stuck-up star; but Beijing's teeny-boppers thought otherwise. About a dozen or so star-struck young women were waiting for hours outside the gate of the film lot in the cold to catch a glimpse of their idol and snap pictures of him with their smart phones. Sadly, Li Yifeng has since been knocked from his pedestal after being detained for soliciting prostitutes in 2022. "Canceling" famous people who are regarded as setting a bad example for society happens in China occasionally.

After the production team returned from filming for six weeks in New York City, I was asked back on set to film my scene.

Jackie and I took turns sitting on a camp chair Jackie had brought, whiling away the time as productively as we could.

TAMMY TREICHEL

We napped, ate the greasy box lunches served on film sets, and of course, practiced my lines until I would be called to shoot my scene. Indeed, waiting is a big and far less glorious part of filming.

After waiting for hours on end with no call for action, eventually I was told the director had decided to do my part with a Chinese actor instead. This happens in the film industry all the time, Jackie told me, actors are replaced or parts are written out or changed at a moment's notice, often without disclosing to the actors why this was being done. That's the way the cookie crumbles! Although I was disappointed that my time on set did not yield any creative result, my acting stint did have a silver lining: Jackie and I met a real-life "Cookie" on the film lot, a wonderful big Husky dog that comforted me with a lick on the face. A photo Jackie took of that encounter is now hanging on my mother's refrigerator back in Washington, D.C.

In Beijing's acting world, when a door closes, a window opens somewhere else — if one searches hard enough. Fate would have another chance in store for me to play a role in a TV series several months later: I was offered the part of a university teacher in a TV series called *Ivy Monsters* (藤科动物也凶猛), about the life of Chinese overseas students at an Ivy League university, which explains the rather bizarre English name, I suppose. My first scene was shot in Huairou, in the suburbs of Beijing, on an actual university campus made up to look as if it was in the US with many English signs, and there were many real foreign students featured as extras.

I had several lines in English that involved instructing the students to do a sociology assignment. Similar to our experience on the set of *I'm Waiting for You in Beijing*, while we were waiting for me to shoot my scene, Jackie and I practiced my lines, and snacked and napped together with some other actors who were playing bit parts. This was what Jackie called "leading a *beipiao* (Beijing drifter) life," and he was relishing the experience while reliving the start of his acting career with me.

Unfortunately, the film crew were behind schedule with the shooting so they couldn't do my scene that day. But they did another brief scene with my calling the leading lady, playing a student, out of the classroom because she was suspected of cheating on an exam. The leading lady was a well-known actress in China called Xu Lu (徐璐).

My scene was done after four or five takes. The director was satisfied; a film crew member said another foreign actress who had been recruited to play a teacher had to do seventy takes until it was a wrap. The director's assistant, a woman, was rough and manhandled some of the extras and yelled when things didn't go smoothly, so that sort of environment steeled my nerves and encouraged me—or rather pushed me—to try to get my scene right in as few takes as possible.

Despite the somewhat stressful environment and ever-changing demands, I managed to keep my cool and tried my best to be polite, professional and adaptable, only then would you be called back for more acting stints. If you prove to be difficult, word might get around in Beijing's acting world, which was smaller than it appeared, and you wouldn't be cast again. Jackie told me to avoid a sense of entitlement, or 公主病 (*gongzhubing*, literally "princess syndrome") at any cost while on a film set. He is very insightful and has a good grasp of who I am as a person, so he might have sensed I have tendencies in that direction.

Also, I learned more about my weaknesses—for example, I needed to speak more loudly and clearly, despite the use of large microphones that were held in front of you and tiny bug-sized ones that you carried on you, concealed under your clothes. So every time I do an acting stint, I improve on something; acting stints are great to hone your skills, learn new ones and build character, something that is usually said of team sports; and in a sense, acting is a bit like playing team sports. After I was done with my scene, Jackie high-fived me and observed, "You have made progress."

As we were taking the subway home, Jackie was pulling a small suitcase with a change of clothes and my large shoes for me in it with one hand, and clasping my hand with his other. "I am holding my dream in one hand, and my love in the other," he mused.

Roughly two weeks later, I was called back to do my second and final scene in *Ivy Monsters*; this time my lines were changed: I was playing the same role, a faculty member/teacher who suspects the leading lady, played by Xu Lu, of cheating on her SATs, the American college entrance exam. Usually great care is taken that one person is cast in one role only in a TV series or movie, or else you might be recognized by the audience as playing multiple roles and that would make everything less credible; one could say this would break the fourth wall by jolting viewers out of the fictional universe. The scene appeared to be set in the US, but we filmed my part in a film lot/art zone in Shunyi, a district on the outskirts of Beijing, in a room decorated to look like an office.

I was immediately attracted to the film lot's retro-style charm; it reminded me of the Bayi Film Lot: An old locomotive was parked on railroad tracks, and there was a Beijing Railway Station complete with a waiting room and benches, and some ad replicas for cigarettes and a Lincoln car in 1930s and 1940s style. I also saw an overturned fishing boat. Jackie said he had visited the lot several years ago for a stint as an extra.

After our arrival, Jackie and I were ushered into a tent within a building, which was supplied with electricity via generators.

HUTONG HEARTTHROBS

Inside the tent were racks of clothes for the leading lady and two simple makeup tables with mirrors. I wore the same clothes I had worn for the first scene; they were my own: a black suit and a pearl necklace. It was important in this case that the clothes, accessories and even hairstyle matched the last scene exactly. That's why photos are occasionally taken of the actors before they shoot a scene, to ensure consistency. Jackie summed up my appearance as "handsome."

This time, I had a different makeup artist who did not concentrate that much on her job and kept humming to herself absentmindedly. She complained to a fellow makeup artist about someone's pimples and told me my thick, curly hair was very awkward to style after pulling at it clumsily with a curling iron, at some point almost burning my ears with it and then blowing on my hair with her mouth. After applying some makeup (she didn't use any mascara or lipstick on me, whereas the makeup artist who had styled me for the first scene had), she told me I should lightly apply my own lipstick.

Luckily, I had an expensive, "Chinese red" lipstick stashed in my purse that Jackie had once arranged for me for special events, and applied some although the shade was different from what I had worn in my first scene. This time, the lipstick color was so striking that my lips were the first thing you noticed about my face. When the makeup artist saw the result, she told me to wipe it off immediately and that she would lightly apply some pinkish, less dramatic-looking lipstick. Why she hadn't done so in the first place if she had the right shade of lipstick in her makeup kit all along seemed neither logical nor efficient.

Jackie said that my Chinese red lipstick was too distracting, viewers would focus on it instead of the leading lady, that's why I was told to take it off; after all, I was only a supporting character. Of course, my vermilion lipstick might not have been so suitable for a teacher, either. Jackie advised me to be polite to the makeup artists, even if they were bitchy, as they could make you look less attractive for the camera if you made them unhappy.

Although I felt tempted to tell the makeup artist what I really thought of her efforts, or rather, lack of them, common sense dictated that I again listen to Jackie. When in China, I try to take Chinese people's advice on how to navigate their society as they usually have a better grasp of the situation; after all, how to handle conflicts is not always the same in China as it is back home and as a foreigner you are always in the weaker position. Plus, some things are simply not worth butting heads over, so pick your fights carefully. I swallowed my pride and decided to concentrate on the task at hand — going over my lines again.

That day, I noticed there were many East Europeans and Africans playing extras, either faculty members or students, and they were discouraged from talking while in the makeup tent and from loitering around there. Those actors with lines, however, could stay, marking a clear difference in treatment. That's how Jackie and I met Darren, an American actor who was selected to play a faculty supervisor. He had been in China for twelve years and had traveled around the country, doing acting stints as a hobby, not to make a living; his main line of work was running an IT company. Darren had been in roughly three hundred movies, playing a wide variety of roles from policemen to ambassadors.

Like me, Darren had brought his own clothes and had some English lines. "Their English translations are kind of funky; it makes the lines harder to memorize," Darren remarked. I knew how he felt; some poor translations from the Chinese didn't roll off the tongue and were thus harder to remember. But Darren had been in China long enough to know that for reasons of face, correcting the set translator's odd English, at least in public, was a bad idea.

    Darren had brought his own camp chair with a self-promotional patch on it bearing the Chinese characters of his name, 达人 (*Da ren*), which coincidentally translates as "expert" or "master." A seasoned actor, Darren had also brought a suitcase with his own snacks. When it was lunch time, Darren opted out of the meal boxes and chewed on a steamed bun instead, while Jackie and I joined most of the crew in eating the fare served in the meal boxes that are standard on film sets. The movie stars eat separately, probably different, better fare, often in their trailers parked on the studio lot.

    The meal boxes are partitioned plastic trays containing rice, vegetables, perhaps eggs and tomatoes, and a bit of meat, e.g., a drumstick, or in this case meatballs, and occasionally steamed buns are served on the side. Sometimes the food for film crews is doled out of vats and onto trays, canteen- or military-style, and is rationed to one meal per person; sometimes you can get seconds or if you have the appetite for it, thirds. The meal boxes do not arouse my enthusiasm, but they do help sustain you over long hours on the set. While Jackie wolfs down his fare with a good appetite and what seems to be enjoyment every time, I try to gulp down mine as fast as possible, making sure the food doesn't linger in my mouth so I don't have to taste it.

    Darren, Jackie and I bonded a bit over lunch and Darren shared several anecdotes from the unpredictable acting industry with us, anecdotes that many actors may find déjà vu occurrences. For example, when playing a warrior, he had to speak some Chinese lines he had difficulty memorizing, so he was allowed to use cue cards, and when he played an ambassador, no one told him he had any lines until they were actually filming. The film crew then squeezed a long script into his hand and gave him thirty minutes to memorize it.

TAMMY TREICHEL

Darren appeared to meet such challenges head-on, enthusiastically and with a sense of humor, to which Jackie and I instinctively responded well. Darren also regarded himself as lucky because of his niche; there did not appear to be many American actors in their 50s and 60s in China. At that age, many Americans had already returned home to a more settled, conventional existence instead of battling it out with visa paperwork and lifestyle as well as cultural differences in China. Talent aside, this gave Darren an edge in playing mature male roles that required native English speakers because there simply wasn't so much competition. The same could be said of American women like me who were over age 40.

After swapping anecdotes with Darren, I was called on set. I was asked to sit down on a sofa after some extras were told to make room for me (I felt somewhat bad about that; everyone was putting in long hours), and Jackie placed my coat over my shoulders while I waited until they got my "office" ready. I felt like a boxer gearing up for a fight.

I peeked into what would be my office, the ring where I expected to fight a battle of nerves against myself. A sign next to my door read "Abby Bauer" (my character's name?) and the interior of my office looked like a generic American office, with its white venetian blinds, English-language tomes, Apple computer, a poster that advertised job training and framed photos of faculty staff that were hung up in seconds after holes were drilled into the walls in my presence.

During our short time together, the director of *Ivy Monsters* struck me as gentle and encouraging. I spoke in Chinese to the director, but when another crew member then spoke to me over a walkie-talkie in what sounded like nearly perfect English, I couldn't understand her! We all laughed, which lightened the mood. It was an unprecedented occurrence; I can only explain it by guessing that I was so focused on the optimal delivery of my English lines while focusing on the director's Chinese requests that my mind temporarily stalled and could not process the new English input.

The leading lady, Xu Lu, entered, wearing a coat draped over her shoulders, and clutching a water bottle to her chest to keep warm (studios can be very cold). She and I were both shown where to stand while delivering our lines, on Xs taped to the floor with duct tape. An assistant came to remove Xu Lu's coat and water bottle, and then it was time for action. "Three, two, one, action!" the director announced, not yelled, in Chinese, and I felt a slight adrenaline rush, but nothing more. I surprised myself by not feeling nervous at all. Perhaps it was the self-confidence from knowing that I was well-prepared and speaking in my mother tongue.

I looked at Xu Lu, the leading lady who was playing the student my character suspected of cheating on her SATs. The actress was petite and had delicate facial features and a quiet, rather innocent air. She was wearing her hair in a bun and a white vest. I tried to give her a reassuring glance because I knew from my Hinton stint how hard it was to recite lines that were not in your native language. I don't know if she caught my glance, but then again, since she was a movie star, I suppose she had little to be afraid of and would be accommodated no matter what happened, after having earned her accolades in the industry.

When delivering my lines, I looked at Xu Lu's forehead, as Jackie had taught me, and let my eyes speak. I was fully present and in the moment, and laser-sharp. I felt more "there" than I usually do in my waking hours. The same could be said of all the subsequent takes. I absolutely loved that feeling of being in a different dimension of reality. Then I was jolted out of that different, crystal clear dimension of reality by the word "咔!"

("*ka*" or "cut").

The director took me aside and said my delivery was good, but he wanted me to deliver the lines again, firmly, but not as fiercely and he wanted the last line to be delivered in a friendlier, more light-hearted fashion after I had looked my counterpart up and down briefly as if assessing her credibility. Of course, as I only had a bit part, there was no way I could have known this as I lacked the context and had not been given the whole script to read, a challenge that actors with small roles such as myself faced.

We then did the scene with the camera shooting from a different angle, and another with me delivering my lines to a yellow X that was made out of duct tape, affixed to the camera and representing Xu Lu's face, while Xu Lu was at my side, reading her lines to me. Everything went unexpectedly well, considering it was my first stint opposite a well-known Chinese actress and in a TV series, which Jackie said have a more hectic pace than movies due to the sheer number of scenes and lines. Jackie looked in from outside the door from time to time, winking at me.

As he had done while I was preparing for my Hinton role, Jackie practiced rigorously with me before the *Ivy Monsters* stint at home, and said when we were done filming that I had done a great job. I think he meant it as he hadn't shied away from constructively criticizing me when I was practicing and making all kinds of rookie mistakes. Truthfully, as with my other acting gigs, it wouldn't have gone so smoothly without his tutoring and encouragement. Next to the trick of looking at the other actor's forehead, he had also warned me to expect different scenarios and different ways a fellow actor could deliver the lines, as well as improvisations, which in no way should throw you off balance or deter you from properly delivering your lines.

HUTONG HEARTTHROBS

Jackie also said that the scene in the faculty office could have been played sitting or standing, and that I should be prepared for both. It turned out that Xu Lu and I were both standing, whereas when I was at home, I had always pictured myself sitting at my desk, hands folded and looking quite strict and superior. I loved the way these acting stints let my imagination run wild and then, when I got down to doing them, clear my mind and fully focus on the task at hand. It was a most cathartic experience every time, perhaps akin to how you feel during meditating.

After Jackie and I returned home, I felt a quick surge of triumph mixed with humility. I posted a few photos of our adventure on WeChat, with my words having a Confucian ring to them as the philosopher believed that among three people, at least one can function as a teacher: "Fun day doing an acting stint in Shunyi, and very happy to meet Darren, a seasoned American actor. Thanks to Jackie for your ongoing support [insert a heart emoji here]. We all sometimes assume the role of students, sometimes of teachers. Today I was both."

12

DREAM A LITTLE DREAM

Jackie and I encourage each other in our various projects. His success is my success, and vice versa; we are always partners, never rivals.

While working on a Jackie Chan movie called *Bleeding Steel* (机器之血) in 2016, my Jackie met a French actor called Anthony (Tony) Gavard. Tony was very warm and supportive of Jackie from the outset, and when he wrote a film script he wanted to direct, he approached Jackie to play opposite himself.

"Tony had insisted he wanted Jackie in the role of the sports teacher," Tony's Chinese wife, Fu Hong (傅红), who has adopted the romantic English/French name Juliet, told me. I followed up with Tony in the months leading up to the filming, and encouraged Jackie to take the role, which would allow him to show his mettle in a comedy with a bit of action and romance rolled in.

Initially Jackie felt the role was too much of a responsibility, but I reassured him by saying I thought he was up to the task, given his experience, good work ethic and talent. "At first I said no because I had never played a big part before," Jackie remembered. "I was afraid I would blow it for the director. Fortunately, Tammy gave me encouragement, she said to accept it, accept it, and always gave me confidence."

So Jackie and I went over the film script together, sometimes seated outside in our hutong house courtyard, with my playing various roles and Jackie responding with his lines. I tried to coach him as best I could, and when I didn't understand the Chinese characters in the script, Jackie would teach them to me. When he was alone, he would go to the canal near our home to practice his lines. So under what Jackie called a high pressure environment, he was able to remember his lines.

In my opinion, a good actor is not only mentally and physically strong, but has the sensitivity and empathy that is needed to put him- or herself in someone else's shoes. I believe Jackie has what it takes.

In July 2018, I visited Quzhou, Zhejiang province, to watch Jackie act in 疯狂的外教 (literally, *Crazy Foreign Teacher* in English). The French title was *Le Laowaï* (*laowai* means foreigner in Chinese, so the French title translates into *The Foreigner*; however, *Welcome to China* was the official English title). Zhejiang province is a well-known place for Chinese movie-making, and home to Hengdian, China's Hollywood, or "Chinawood."

The movie is about a French sports teacher called Anthony who goes to a local Quzhou school as part of an exchange program. During his stint at the school, he befriends the local Chinese staff, among them a sports teacher, played by Jackie, who has the same name in the film. Anthony introduces the French sport of pétanque to Jackie the sports teacher and the whole school and excites his Chinese hosts about the sport, which involves throwing metal balls toward a target ball on a court.

The film is a comedy about East-meets-West and intercultural friendship that is fostered through sports. Despite initial slip-ups and cross-cultural misunderstandings, Anthony eventually forges close ties to the local Chinese community.

The film was written and directed by Anthony (Tony), who plays the main role, the eponymous French sports teacher. His Chinese wife in real life, Fu Hong, also played a key role in making the movie, which could be called the couple's joint dream and they made a lot of personal sacrifices to make it happen.

The film employed some local talents, e.g., Fu Hong, who is from Quzhou, doubled as an actress who plays Lili (莉莉), a teacher who is enamored of all things French and becomes Jackie's love interest. She and Jackie make Anthony feel at home in China and with Chinese culture before—spoiler alert!— getting married at the end of the film. Fu Hong graciously said she hoped I didn't mind her "marrying" Jackie in the movie.

"Jackie is funny; he is always so shy," Fu Hong remarked about their interactions on set. When she was choosing her wedding dress for the scene, Jackie and I held a video chat, with Jackie sheepishly peeking out behind various dresses. Yes, Jackie could be very assertive or very shy, depending on the context.

I found Fu Hong to be a warm-hearted, incredibly smart and also insightful person. "A cross-cultural relationship requires a lot of sacrifice," she said. As someone who had a foreign spouse, she knew what she was talking about; she and Tony are now living in Paris, so it is harder for her to see her family in Quzhou. Moreover, she said it could be hard for a Western woman to be married to a Chinese man because Chinese society is more traditional.

"I do wish you have a good future, you see, China is beautiful, and a Chinese boy is loving you; I am happy for you and Jackie!" Fu Hong told me. Living in a foreign country can be exciting but also entail suffering; after all in life, you have to make your choices and set priorities.

And after I had departed for Beijing to get back to my job, with Jackie staying behind to work on the film, she assured me, "We will take care of your man, do not worry!"

As for the other local talents besides Fu Hong, a teacher at the high school acted as the father of one of the students who in typical Chinese fashion was displeased that his daughter was more interested in pétanque than her math studies and argues with her on the sports field. Some of the high schoolers were also cast in the movie wearing their school uniforms.

A Frenchman called Benoit had been flown in from France to do the camera work. Benoit used to be a Broadway ballet dancer in his younger years. He had a laid-back style and worked barefoot, despite the rain puddles and soft caterpillars underfoot, obviously enjoying his Chinese surroundings. He nicknamed the film camera "Cosette" after the waif-like character in *Les Misérables* because the camera needed a lot of care; for example, it couldn't overheat in the hot summer temperatures, otherwise, it would stop working. Tony, as the director, gave some instructions in French, which made me feel I was at a cultural crossroads with Chinese, French and English on the set. I sat back and enjoyed the interplay between different languages.

TAMMY TREICHEL

I admired the on-camera chemistry between Tony and the Chinese actors, with this creative project bringing East and West closer together during the course of several weeks. Jackie told me he was excited to be acting opposite a foreigner for the first time and was intrigued by Tony's hands-on, do-it-yourself approach. For example, on the sports field a heel of Tony's shoe fell off. Instead of changing into a new pair of shoes, Tony insisted on going about his work in the scorching heat with his broken shoe. "This was the first time since I started acting that I saw a sight like this: a foreign director insisting on doing things himself on set; I was very touched and inspired to strive hard and do a good job acting," Jackie told me earnestly.

When I visited the set for several days, we were mainly filming at the school. It was the first time for me to visit a Chinese dormitory (the school accepts boarders), complete with four wooden bunk beds and numbered stools in each room. I also ate some meals in the school canteen and was intrigued by the metal trays, which reminded me of my student days in Heidelberg. Finally, I enjoyed talking to the students, whose English was exceptional, considering their limited interactions with foreigners.

One student showed me the edition of the American literary classic F. Scott Fitzgerald's *The Great Gatsby* they were studying in English class, and he admitted it was a challenge for him because of the vocabulary. He read the sentences over and over, he said. For Jackie, the school atmosphere brought back happy memories of his own school days.

I enjoyed the Quzhou No. 2 High School's beautiful grounds, lush vegetation and Chinese pond herons flapping through the trees. An English teacher at the school told me, "You can feel the harmony between humans and nature when staying here." The same could largely be said about the different cultures interacting on set.

Whereas most foreigners can be found either working or traveling in China's first-tier cities such as Beijing, Shanghai or Guangzhou, I love exploring China's smaller cities such as Quzhou, and venturing where quite not as many foreigners do. It is the luxury of an expat life in China to have some extra time to see what smaller Chinese cities are like, and I am grateful that being invited to a movie set allowed me to travel to Quzhou.

When not on the set, Jackie and I had the time to take a blitz tour of the Quzhou Museum and the local Confucius Temple, where I admired the southern Chinese garden scenery defined by water, fed the ravenous koi, and marveled at the potted orchids, heavy wooden furniture and well-executed oil paintings of Confucius' life. Jackie told me he loved the interplay between water, plants and history in the city.

Indeed, discovering what smaller cities have to offer can be quite a special experience—but not just for me, also for the locals involved. Silas, a British expat who managed a bar in one of Quzhou's picturesque bar streets, was very friendly and waved from behind the bar counter when Jackie and I passed his establishment. Although we were strangers, there was a sense of recognition between us, maybe because Silas and I were both foreigners. It was late so we didn't stay for drinks or a snack, but I did enjoy chatting with Silas about what it was like running a bar as a foreigner in China and the challenges involved.

Silas' bar offered Western fare such as tiramisu, brownies and sausages off the grill, and there was table football; the Western elements blended in well with the traditional Chinese surroundings. Star cut-outs were suspended from the ceiling.

Silas, who sported a trendy man bun, came out and sat on the window sill of his bar, legs crossed, while I stood. Warm light emanated from his bar through the window, making the outside glow. His Chinese was fluent after having spent many years in China and he appeared to be quite rooted in the local culture; Jackie said that judging by our conversation, even his thinking had become as complex as that of a Chinese.

Except for Silas, I didn't spot a single other foreigner off set in Quzhou. Silas had said there was an expat community, but to me, they remained invisible. As in Luoyang or other smaller Chinese cities I had visited, people tended to stare at me on the streets and even in Quzhou's Starbucks, where I made a furtive exit with my Caffè Americano because I felt self-conscious. One local woman just stared at me open-mouthed when I asked her for directions in Chinese, then finally replied after she had recovered from her surprise.

Once the locals had understood I was able to communicate with them, most of them were quite friendly, including the owners of the guesthouse where I was staying. Most guesthouses, which offer more simple amenities than hotels, do not accept foreigners in China, but I had found one that did. It was an ideal place for me to lay down my head and the location was excellent, only ten minutes away on foot from Quzhou No. 2 High School. Although water was plentiful with all the rains, it was ironic that I had to wait twenty minutes for a trickle of hot water to come out of the guesthouse shower nozzle. Still, the simple guesthouse had the trappings of a Chinese hotel I enjoy—a water kettle and plastic hotel slippers, which I borrowed on one occasion to wade through the rains to the film set and back. Meanwhile, Jackie was living in the men's dorms with other male members of the film crew, always on call.

Because of his work, Jackie couldn't pick me up at the high-speed railway station or see me off there when I left for Beijing, which made him feel a bit guilty, so I had to take cabs to and from the train station myself. Since this was in broad daylight, I felt safe doing so. Jackie later described my presence on the film set as "comforting and warm" to him. And when I left for the Quzhou high-speed railway station, Jackie waved goodbye as I was speeding off in a cab, but he could rest assured that I was waiting for him in the hutong house when he returned to Beijing. We would always wait for each other.

∽∽∽

As luck would have it, I was there during the film launch ceremony of *Le Laowaï* in Quzhou. The film launch saw the investors dropping by, as well as the school head, and some celebrities had sent in videotaped messages to be shown at the ceremony, wishing the film success. Now it was at the film launch that Jackie and I met an acquaintance who would later introduce us to a very special lady in Beijing.

Zhang Weixin (张伟欣) was a famous actress in 1980s China. Her daughter, Li Xiaolu (李小璐, Jacqueline Li) is an accomplished film and TV series actress in her own right and was the youngest actress at age sixteen to win the Golden Horse Award for Best Leading Actress in China (the Chinese equivalent of an Oscar). I later saw Li Xiaolu play the lead in the 2006 TV series *Calling Love* (来电奇缘), a humble young country girl from Hunan who falls in love with a 高富帅 (*gaofushuai,* or "tall, rich and handsome man," the proverbial Mr. Perfect in China and in other countries as well). Although the plot was rather predictable in that it was just another modern-day Cinderella story, I did enjoy Li Xiaolu's not just being another pretty face, but endowing the role with some spunk.

Zhang Weixin invited Jackie and me to a New Year's Party on the second day of the Lunar New Year in 2019. Despite Zhang Weixin's family's status, I got the impression that she was very humble and radiated inner tranquility. Zhang Weixin was soft-spoken and spoke good English. At the party, her daughter Li Xiaolu put in a brief appearance wearing a baseball cap and white down jacket and politely extended her greetings to the guests. Li Xiaolu reminded me of a gentle snowfall when she appeared, coming suddenly but quickly changing the atmosphere with her presence, making it magical. I could sense the other guests were wowed by her presence.

"She is shy," Zhang Weixin said of her daughter.

I very much admire persons who are outgoing and quite the dynamo, as Jackie could be at times. Yet I was moved by the humility, hospitality and a sense of class shown by Zhang Weixin and her family when we were guests in their home; clearly, their success had not gone to their heads. I feel very fortunate Jackie and I were able to meet them in person.

———∞∞∞———

Jackie's idol and English namesake is Jackie Chan—when it came to deciding between the English name "Steve," which he had encountered frequently in TV series and found quite tasteful and gentlemanly, or "Jackie," it was a no-brainer for him (many Chinese are in the habit of choosing an English name for themselves, whereas foreigners in China might choose a Chinese one to facilitate communication and to a certain extent immersion into the local culture). So "Jackie" it was! And when he met foreigners on the street, Jackie had the funny habit of pulling out a photo of himself with Jackie Chan on a movie set, pointing at the superstar and saying "Jackie Chan," then pointing at himself and saying, "No Jackie Chan."

We watched the Jackie Chan blockbusters *Rumble in the Bronx* (1995) and *Rush Hour* (1998) together, as well as some of Jackie Chan's newer films, and I must say I mostly prefer the older Jackie Chan movies, with the exception of perhaps the 2019 movie *The Climbers* (see below), because in my opinion, the older Jackie Chan films are more focused on characters and plots and more realistic instead of exploding with special effects. Then again, my Jackie was a part of Jackie Chan's newer movies, so of course I continue to watch them too when they are released.

My Jackie has worked as a credited stand-in for some of Jackie Chan's movies. A stand-in is someone who bears a varying degree of resemblance to a big star and "stands in" while lights and cameras are being readied or even substitutes in some scenes, e.g., where shots of hands or legs are needed or in long-distance shots, where a superstar's face isn't visible. This facilitates a superstar's work and also saves the production team time and money (a big star's time is of course very expensive; having a stand-in do some of the work is a lot cheaper).

When Jackie was growing up in the countryside, he was crazy about Jackie Chan movies, especially *Rush Hour*, which he has watched about a hundred times. But never in a million years did he imagine he would one day meet—and work together with—his big-screen idol.

Fortune smiled on Jackie when he finally got his foot in the acting door by inadvertently landing the role of a cook in the movie *The 1911 Revolution* (辛亥革命), a historical drama, which was incidentally also Jackie Chan's 100th movie. The movie was released in 2011.

From then on, Jackie has worked together with Jackie Chan on several occasions as a credited stand-in. He was Jackie Chan's stand-in in the movies *Skiptrace* (绝地逃亡, 2016) as well as *Railroad Tigers* (铁道飞虎, 2016). Later there was *Kung Fu Yoga* (功夫瑜伽, 2017) and a sunglasses commercial, among others. And work for *Bleeding Steel* (机器之血), which hit movie screens in 2017, took Jackie to Sydney, Australia, in 2016.

TAMMY TREICHEL

In Australia, the *Bleeding Steel* crew filmed at the Sydney Opera House, and a scene was set on the roof of the Opera House and around the stairs outside the iconic building. In one shot, the crew were shooting on the outer stairs of the building, and my Jackie had to run from the upper stairs to the lowermost ones. They used a stopwatch to calculate the time it took for Jackie to run from the top to the bottom of the stairs. After they had calculated the time, Jackie then had to turn left and run back. Then they asked Jackie to jump on a yacht and see how much time it took him to do that. Thus, the film crew measured the difference between the filming plan and the situation after the live drill.

On set, Jackie also met the Australian actress Tess Haubrich, who has been in many international productions and played the "Woman in Black," a villain, in *Bleeding Steel*. "Wow, she was so tall!" Jackie remembered. (Haubrich, also a model, reportedly stands a majestic 1.80 meters or 5'10" tall.) A far cry from his short little foreign "goody two-shoes" girlfriend Tammy, indeed...

More recently, my Jackie was recruited as a stand-in for a gripping Jackie Chan/Wu Jing (吴京) movie called *The Climbers* (攀登者), which is based on the true story of a group of Chinese mountaineers successfully reaching the peak of Mount Everest from the treacherous north side in 1960 and 1975. The scenes my Jackie was involved in were shot near Tianjin in artificial snow, not too far from Mount Pan, a mountain I had mentioned before which Jackie and I had also hiked. A photo of my Jackie depicted several people on set assisting him with getting into the orange outdoor gear the Everest climbers wore, and he said it was hellish to use the restroom while wearing it, especially for the women.

Indeed, every time he has worked as a stand-in for Jackie Chan, it was a completely different experience for my Jackie. However, when *The Climbers* hit the big screen on National Day of 2019, on the 70th founding anniversary of the People's Republic of China, together with other patriotic movies, I was there to watch it with him, holding his hand and in feverish excitement, as I did every time one of the movies my Jackie had participated in came out. Occasionally, I would also catch Jackie wiping away some tears.

Work for *Skiptrace* took Jackie to Inner Mongolia and Yangshuo (阳朔) and San Jiang (三江) in the Guangxi Zhuang Autonomous Region, and *Railroad Tigers* took him to Liaoning province's Diaobingshan (调兵山), which has many old railway cars. Jackie vividly remembers watching the animated movie *An American Tail* in his hotel room in Diaobingshan and being enchanted by the movie's stirring music and the mice called Fievel and Tanya who are following their dreams to a better life, which reminded him of the two of us and brought tears to his eyes.

On the set of *Railroad Tigers*, my Jackie briefly told Jackie Chan about me, his foreign girlfriend. Jackie Chan responded by asking, "What language(s) does she speak?" But before my Jackie could respond, he was called back to work.

When acting as a stand-in for Jackie Chan in a sunglasses commercial, he traveled to Shanghai for it. Meanwhile, *Bleeding Steel* saw my Jackie going to Australia and Taiwan for several months, and his shots in the movie showing the Chinese mountaineers' ascent of Mount Everest in *The Climbers* were actually filmed near Tianjin (you can see my Jackie from the back as he is climbing "Mount Everest" towards the end of the movie). Meanwhile, his part in *Kung Fu Yoga* was shot in Beijing, and I was graciously allowed to visit the set for a day (more later).

Jackie has a lot to thank Jackie Chan for. "If it weren't for Jackie Chan, I wouldn't have come to Beijing and met you," he has told me on several occasions (and the same could be said of the Beijing subway, which served as our actual matchmaker). I for one thank the Jackie Chan team for giving my Jackie the opportunity to go to Australia and Taiwan for *Bleeding Steel*. Going to Australia was Jackie's first trip abroad and a truly eye-opening experience for him. I got to travel to Australia vicariously by following his adventures via WeChat video; I had never been there myself.

I clearly remember the day Jackie was scheduled to fly to Australia. While sitting on his side of the bed in our hutong house shortly after waking up, Jackie suddenly burst into tears. He said he was concerned about leaving me alone for about three months, and what about cooking and my getting nutritious meals? Although initially alarmed, I was able to comfort Jackie quickly, gently hugged and kissed him and said this would be an exciting, once-in-a-lifetime experience for him and that time would pass quickly. I did not want to stand in the way of this opportunity and would be fine by myself in Beijing for several months, I assured him.

It must have been an exciting yet also very stressful experience for Jackie to go abroad alone for the first time; like many Chinese, he had never left the Mainland before (by comparison, I took my first transatlantic flight on my father's lap from Washington, D.C., to Germany at the tender age of three, so I was a seasoned globe trotter). Also, I received assurances from my emergency contact in the film crew that they would take good care of my Jackie, which they did.

Roughly 24 hours after his departure, my smart phone started buzzing; Jackie wanted to connect with me via WeChat video. I was happy to see him beaming back at me from the Southern Hemisphere. His journey had gone smoothly thanks to a flight attendant who had filled out the immigration and customs forms for him, and a Chinese whom he had followed through immigration and customs before being picked up by someone from the film crew at Arrivals.

After getting over his fear of going out, he eventually left his hotel after several days and made friends with some overseas Chinese in Sydney, namely a college student who would help him navigate Sydney's subway system and take him on day trips, and a kind, elderly lady who would invite him for several hamburgers at KFC and take him to see the koalas at Sydney's Taronga Zoo.

From Taronga Zoo, Jackie sent me some footage of koalas chewing on eucalyptus leaves. As for the kangaroos, Jackie reported that they were mostly sleeping. Before he departed for Australia, I had already told him about Australia's amazing nature and culture—koalas, kangaroos and indigenous people—to make the trip even more palatable. I was initially surprised Jackie did not really appear to know about these things before, but considering he grew up in China's countryside and had never left China before, it was not so surprising after all.

Jackie told me how impressed he was by the politeness of the locals; a policewoman had been very helpful to him and the Australians held doors open for him, to which he replied in his best English with a gracious "Thank you, sir" or "Thank you, madam."

He bought an oil painting from a street painter showing a little girl in a blue hoodie leading a large dog, which looked like a St. Bernard—he said the blond, tomboyish girl reminded him of me—and gave some money to a beggar and his dog. In a park, he chanced upon a man standing on a soapbox, dressed in 19th century-style clothes and a top hat, and giving a speech. When Jackie asked me what the man was doing, I found it difficult to explain, as "soapboxing" is not an activity that Chinese engage in and there was no equivalent Chinese word.

Jackie also liked to pet the dogs tied up in front of the supermarket near the service apartments which had been rented by the film crew. It was there that he prepared the Chinese Valentine's Day surprise I had already mentioned: having various Australians pose with his hand-written sign that said, "宝贝我爱你 ~ Baby I love you ~ 七夕快乐 ~ Happy Chinese Valentine's Day."

It was at that supermarket that Jackie admired the self-checkout kiosks as he had never seen those before, and bought himself a lot of milk because he thought it was cheap and tasty, as well as hamburger buns, yogurt, spaghetti noodles, ketchup and frozen pizzas that he would pull out of the oven of his service apartment, half-burned. Jackie even bought himself an avocado but didn't take a fancy to its taste and discarded it, half-eaten. Like many Chinese who go abroad, he found the Western diet to be a bit rough on his body, with his developing what in traditional Chinese medicine is called an excess of "internal heat" (*shanghuo* or 上火), so I helped Jackie buy some medicine from a pharmacist, with me visible on camera and translating via WeChat video. I doubt the pharmacist ever saw a customer making a purchase in that manner before.

Entering the building where his service apartment was, Jackie was unaccustomed to the revolving door of his building, and he ran into it the first time. He found the rotation direction of the doors in Australia was the opposite from that in China so when he went through the door, he felt a little dizzy. Back in the apartment, Jackie was intrigued by a toaster and an espresso machine and asked me what the appliances were for and took his first bubble bath, or actually even first bath, in a bathtub, as most Chinese just use showers. He turned on the TV to watch and listen to some English-language programming but soon turned it off again. He admitted it was all quite unfamiliar; he must have felt what I did when I first came to China — culture shock.

We both experimented with Jackie filming a flushing toilet as I wondered if the water really drained in the opposite direction in the Southern Hemisphere (our results were inconclusive, but it should, according to the Coriolis effect; supposedly, a toilet bowl is too small to observe this effect). While it was summer for me in China, in the Northern Hemisphere, it was winter in Australia and got dark early, so Jackie did not stay out late.

After Australia, Jackie and some of the *Bleeding Steel* film crew left for China again and went to Taipei. In Taiwan, he was intrigued by the number of motorcycles and had to work as a stand-in in a Jackie Chan motorcycle scene. On his days off, Jackie toured the National Palace Museum and Sun Yat-sen Memorial Hall. When he returned home after three months of working as a stand-in, Jackie brought a suitcase of playful-looking clothes that he had bought at a discount for me after making friends with a shopkeeper in Taiwan. Indeed, a man returning from a business trip with a suitcase full of new clothes for his "lady" is a dream come true for many women!

Back in Beijing, an unforgettable experience for me was being invited to visit the set of *Kung Fu Yoga* when Jackie was working as a stand-in for Jackie Chan, and watching the superstar and director Stanley Tong (唐季礼) at work together. Here are my impressions of "rubbing shoulders with Jackie Chan."

Kung Fu Yoga is an action-adventure comedy film. Shooting took place in different locations such as India and Iceland, as well as in the penthouse of a high-end hotel in Beijing. As a guest on the penthouse film set, I was given an ID card similar to the ones Jackie Chan's staff were wearing. The film set was well hidden behind the facade of a wellness center. At the entrance, there was a reception desk staffed with nurses. I asked my Jackie whether the nurses were fake (my logic was that they were there to deflect attention from what was going on in the rooms behind them). To my surprise, he said the nurses were actually real—on standby in case someone got injured on the set.

It was there, in a hidden enclave, that I received one of the most passionate kisses ever from my Jackie. During a break, we snuck into the enclave; the nurses were nowhere to be seen... He pulled me close... it appeared as if electrifying passion was being transmitted to me, passion for each other, passion for life, passion for the moment... We felt young, naughty and full of vigor. No one discovered us, the nurses stayed away, and when it was time for Jackie to go back to work, we were suddenly prim and proper again...

The penthouse was a duplex, and on the first floor there was living room furniture, Tang dynasty-style woodcuts and books on shelves. There was catering on a dining room table for the staff with a kitchen area. The general atmosphere was like that of a casual Friday night party in a private home.

Upstairs were props used in different movies, e.g., a wooden Buddha and the scroll painting from Jackie Chan's movie *The Myth* (神话, 2005), a film that was also directed by Stanley Tong and combines martial arts, adventure, fantasy and romance. The scroll painting features *The Myth's* Korean princess, Ok-Soo, who generally cuts an unhappy, sulking figure in the movie and only smiles for the person painting her portrait when she catches sight of the Qin-dynasty Chinese general Meng Yi (played by Jackie Chan), whom she loves and waits for patiently in perpetuity.

Interestingly, that particular Jackie Chan movie held a special place in my Jackie's heart; Jackie once confided to me that it was the movie *The Myth* that had given him the strength and faith to persevere and wait for me until I had returned to China from the US back in 2015. Well, fortunately, my Jackie didn't have to wait quite as long as Ok-Soo for a reunion with his lover! Also, there were framed photos of Jackie Chan in different movies on a shelf. Jackie Chan's two bicycles were strapped to the banisters of the stairs connecting the two stories of the duplex.

Shooting for *Kung Fu Yoga* took place downstairs. There was equipment everywhere, film cameras, a big microphone, screens for the A and B cameras, dollies, straps and hoists used for stunts, and so on. Dozens of people were on the set: cameramen, makeup artists, assistants and stand-ins, who were either lounging on or hovering about the set like butterflies. There was a beautiful Bollywood star as well who was a bit of a diva; she spoke British English and was wearing a white bathrobe. Yet there was no sign of Jackie Chan when I first arrived.

I was very careful not to get in anyone's way or trip over the wires; the only faux pas I committed was upsetting some books when I first entered. What struck me was that you had to stand a lot, keep quiet during filming and there was absolutely no photo-taking on the set, with signs saying it was not permitted.

The first time I laid eyes on Jackie Chan, he made an imposing appearance, sweeping in right past me around lunch time in a white jogging outfit and black sunglasses. What surprised me was that he was not larger than life, but looked exactly as he did in his movies (I imagined stars to appear different in real life than on the screen, stripped of makeup and costume).

I had the pleasure of shaking director Stanley Tong's hand when I first arrived. Tong and Jackie Chan spoke both Mandarin and Cantonese on set, casually switching between the two. Numerous times, I would hear the director and assistant director shout "rolling," "action" and "咔" ("*ka*" or "cut"); the first two words were spoken in English. One of the assistants had to test the wooden dummy on which Jackie Chan would perform his stunts, appearing like an acrobat in a circus.

Then it was Jackie Chan's turn. I stood only several meters

away from him as he did his takes and was amazed at what he was still physically capable of at the age of sixty plus: Jackie Chan repeatedly punched the dummy, upon which his assistants had applied powder, and did handstands as well. His body was extremely pliable; indeed, Jackie Chan is still known for doing his own stunts in movies.

The first scene involved Jackie Chan entering with a small carton of milk in his hand, looking around mischievously and then proceeding to the dummy. After he was done with his kung fu sessions, an assistant came to hand him a towel with a "Jackie Chan" logo on it to wipe away perspiration (Jackie Chan has his very own clothing line with the same logo featured on T-shirts). Also, another assistant occasionally handed him a brush or applied a tiny bit of makeup on his cheek using a cotton swab.

What struck me was the very respectful attitude of some of his assistants, only natural as he was first, their boss, and second, a big shot, if not a legend, in the entertainment industry. Jackie Chan seemed totally focused on his work; he appeared very serious for someone who could cut the clownish Houdini on screen, always narrowly escaping trouble due to his bag of kung fu tricks and rubber-like body. He truly is a contemporary trickster hero.

When I briefly posted about my adventure on Facebook, an American friend commented, "Super cool! I hope he [Jackie Chan] is not playing the clown in this one." I replied, "We'll see. I was impressed by his super-serious work attitude, though. Didn't smile once the cameras weren't rolling."

A Chinese friend asked whether Jackie Chan looks in real life like he does in the movies. I said yes, and she replied that usually, people look heavier on TV. When she asked me whether he is as famous in the West as he is in China, I again said yes, and added that he is mainly known for kung fu in the US. In China,

HUTONG HEARTTHROBS

Jackie Chan is a big star on many fronts, and in Beijing, Jackie Chan beams back at you from many ads.

Jackie Chan's staff slept very little, I heard, maybe five hours a night, but I suppose something similar could be said of those working in the film industry in general as shooting a movie is an exhausting endeavor. I had gotten a taste of that myself when playing Joan Hinton. It seemed the *Kung Fu Yoga* crew were only filming tiny segments at a time and made slow progress, at least on the day I visited.

However, my Jackie told me that Jackie Chan rewards the film crew for their hard work. He is good to his staff, commemorates their birthdays, poses for photos with them and gives them copies of his memoir, which he autographs individually. "Jackie Chan was very kind to people," my Jackie told me. "He helped the crew to carry props and cleaned the scene. He made sure that there was no garbage on the scene after shooting." I also heard from my Jackie that he hand-feeds crew members grapes...

That struck me as rather strange, but maybe I'll have the good fortune of catching a glimpse of that another time.

When I was visiting the set of *Kung Fu Yoga*, my Jackie made sure that I felt comfortable and introduced me to some of the crew members.

Jackie Chan autographed two copies of the Chinese version of his book *Never Grow Up* for Jackie and me, when my Jackie was working on *Railroad Tigers* with him in Diaobingshan. My Jackie and I greatly treasure our copies. "Dear Tamara, With Love, Enjoy, Jackie Chan," read the inscription in my copy dated 2015-11-6.

I admit I have been a tiny bit jealous of my Jackie's ongoing idolizing of Jackie Chan on occasion. For example, Jackie's parents have set aside an apartment for Jackie in their self-constructed apartment building for use once we get married. Jackie has taken the liberty of decorating it. In the breakfast nook, he had two fabric window blinds custom-made for us. One featured a photo of Jackie and me and the other one was of my Jackie grinning next to his idol Jackie Chan on some movie set. Well, at least it wasn't a supermodel or Playboy Bunny!

Jackie Chan, one could say, has reached the apex of worldwide fame. Conversely, when my Jackie and I were attending an event at some point in Beijing, we met a young British man who had just moved to China from Singapore and appeared to think very highly of himself. When I introduced him to my Jackie, and said that he was an actor, he asked whether Jackie was famous. When I said "no," he abruptly turned away instead of asking Jackie more about his colorful life and perhaps making a new friend. "What a snob!" I thought.

But Jackie and I did have our fifteen minutes of fame. When Jackie was working as a campus security guard at the Guangdong University of Foreign Studies, he achieved some local fame because of his unremitting efforts to study English using the rather unorthodox "Crazy English" method pioneered by the Chinese educator Li Yang (李阳), who focuses on enunciation and building self-confidence in learning English.

Jackie's English-learning efforts together with his helpful attitude towards the university staff and charisma caught the attention of some journalists. China's national broadcaster China Central Television (CCTV) featured him on the news, and a local reporter also wrote a story about him. About ten years later in July 2017, another local reporter wanted to follow up and see what Jackie was up to at that time and wrote a feature story about him, his background, his acting experiences and his meeting me for the "People" (今日人) section in *Guangzhou Daily*.

HUTONG HEARTTHROBS

The story, published in Chinese on July 17/18, 2017, both in print and online, was titled "An Inspiring Story of a Security Guard from Guangdong University of Foreign Studies—He studied English with the utmost effort which led him to a beautiful American girlfriend and a stand-in job for Jackie Chan."

In the story, Jackie talked about meeting Jackie Chan for the first time on the set of *The 1911 Revolution*. He was so nervous, he said, he couldn't breathe. "It's a feeling that nobody can describe as your childhood idol is standing right in front of you," Jackie said in the article. In *The 1911 Revolution*, he played a cook, and Jackie Chan and he had one short scene together. Although it only lasted one second, Jackie felt it had been worth the hardship of spending three months as an unpaid extra in the Bayi Film Lot and being exhausted from distributing about one hundred resumes.

"Acting as a stand-in for Jackie Chan, I was very nervous at first. But Chan was like a big brother, he told me he used to stand in for someone else, too. As a stand-in, I could learn many things," Jackie was quoted in the story as saying.

"Brother Chan is nice to every crew member. He often says that the sky is watching everything we do. He encourages us all the time. I'm really very grateful for he has given me the faith to persevere till today."

About our relationship, Jackie said that he and I both encourage each other. "She (Tammy) thinks that I'm full of positive energy, and she also likes my smile," he said. When the reporter asked Jackie about the pressure he was experiencing in Beijing, Jackie replied, "I believe that opportunities and challenges co-exist. Pressure has become the force driving me forward. My girlfriend and I enjoy the process. The movie and television industry is quite different from others. When I'm busy, I work day and night without resting. However, I'm willing to work as hard as I can, because I haven't studied in a specialized acting school. Starting out as a security guard and then becoming an actor, I'm very grateful."

When asked what his biggest gain was, Jackie replied, "It's the dream that drives me forward… Be brave to dream and courageous to act. The biggest gain from acting is joy. It's a joyful thing to learn from my idol, and also to do what I truly love."

The story, with its combination of a humble Chinese security guard learning some English, finding true love with an American girlfriend, meeting Jackie Chan and trying his luck in the acting industry was a big hit and made headline news for a day or two. When I last checked, the story had gotten over 100,000 reads, 911 likes and numerous comments.

Some of my coworkers in Beijing congratulated me on being in the headlines; I had wrongly assumed that the *Guangzhou Daily*'s reach was local and that they wouldn't read the story. I think perhaps it was the fact that it was "inspiring," as the headline had promised, that attracted so many readers, encouraging others to be "brave to dream and courageous to act," especially in a society that is still largely conformist and traditional. When I asked a Chinese coworker why she thought the *Guangzhou Daily* article was so popular, she replied that Jackie was realizing the dream of some of the grassroots—working on Jackie Chan film sets and having a foreign girlfriend.

Indeed, Jackie had confided to me that he had three dreams: meeting Jackie Chan, having an American girlfriend (Hollywood movies had somehow given him a positive impression of American women and when he was working as a security guard in Guangdong, he had also seen some pretty foreign exchange students, which piqued his interest) and traveling around the world. The third dream is still pending, of course. What's more, Jackie said he would like to help the elderly and children in need as one's personal dreams should also have a public aspect and benefit society, he believed; once you have helped yourself and made your own life better, you are better equipped to help others.

After the *Guangzhou Daily* story was published, a neighbor as well as one of Jackie's fellow gym members immediately recognized Jackie as being the focus of the story. What's more, a stranger approached me on the subway after apparently having read the story and identifying me. And a young woman who worked as a security guard at our local Yonghegong subway station also recognized us after the story circulated on the microblog Sina Weibo, and from that day, we greeted each other in the subway. Interestingly, in a WeChat post she would later write in Chinese, "The Beijing subway carries the weight of the dreams of so many ordinary people," which was true in Jackie's and my case.

This attention was followed by several interview requests for Jackie from leading Chinese news outlets such as 知音 (*Zhiyin*, in English known as *Bosom Friend*), a celebrity/women's magazine that focuses on touching true stories, 读者 (*Duzhe*, literally *Reader*), a well-known, general interest magazine, 财新 (*Caixin*), which mainly focuses on business, and CCTV. Some of these requests actually resulted in stories, e.g., a Sri Lankan journalist from Caixin conducted an interview with Jackie in fluent Chinese that was translated into English and gave a good overview of his acting career and related hardships. CCTV even offered to arrange for us to get married on one of their programs and they would bear the expenses, and although we felt honored, we politely declined for privacy reasons.

A reporter from the Yang County local paper in Jackie's hometown wrote a *Guangzhou Daily* knockoff piece about Jackie and with his permission, pulled all of the photos of Jackie he could find on Jackie's social media accounts, flattering or not, for his story, yet I must say the reporter was always very pleasant to interact with for Jackie and enthusiastically championed his cause against an occasional internet troll. Someone in Jackie's hometown also asked him to be in an advertisement for his newly opened hotpot restaurant. This didn't lead to anything concrete, but Jackie was grateful to be asked.

Truthfully, I felt shy about all the attention, ill at ease initially. For a day or two after the *Guangzhou Daily* story appeared, I was afraid of leaving our hutong house. I may have gotten over my agoraphobia had the small media storm lasted, but that was not something I needed to worry about. Jackie, too, felt overwhelmed, and his left eye started to become sore and inflamed, aggravated by conducting video interviews via his smart phone or computer screens and lack of sleep.

Yes, the story was hot for a day or two, but then the news cycle continues. Common people can become an internet celebrity overnight and just as quickly fade into obscurity; you are a grassroots "star" one day, and the next, China forgets who you are.

But our most memorable interview experience would be with another well-known media organization in China, Xinhua. They would conduct a Livestream and then a mini-documentary with Jackie and me about our "Chinese Dream." For the location, I suggested the Bayi Film Lot in Beijing's Fengtai District. After all, what would be a more suitable location than the cradle of Jackie's acting dream?

In fact, Jackie had already taken me to the Bayi Film Lot once before in 2015, when it was open to tourists. The Bayi Film Lot was used for shooting Chinese war movies. While strolling across the lot, Jackie and I saw some actors portraying Kuomintang soldiers and two actresses playing nurses, and I had my photo taken with one of the nurses, a pretty young woman who appeared rather nervous. Several people were busy preparing new sets, painting buildings or writing Chinese characters on square pieces of paper, or hammering away at wooden structures.

Some of the buildings had Chinese slogans and characters on them, and some were charred from having been actually set on fire for a movie. Most buildings were empty, but I saw one store selling "goods." Some buildings were unlocked, so you could enter, which was not always a rewarding experience as some rooms were trashed and others had mildew on the ceilings, waiting to be done up for use in filming. There was also a "hospital" and a "canteen" for the "soldiers," featuring posters about sanitation on the walls and moldy steamed buns on the counter. What's more, there were fortifications from which the "soldiers" would shoot at their enemies. There was even an entire Japanese camp with a torn Japanese flag, buildings with paper walls and lanterns, as well as trenches, where Jackie said he himself had once lain, shouldering guns while playing a soldier. Movies about the Second Sino-Japanese War (1937-1945) appear to be a staple on Chinese television.

Jackie pointed out the path on which the tanks moved, as well as the office at the main gate of the film lot where he had lived and slept, and the tree underneath which he had eaten lunch when he was embarking on his acting career. It was truly a trip down memory lane for Jackie, and I was intrigued to be strolling down it together with him! He had come full circle.

In August 2017, before shooting the Livestream and minidocumentary at the Bayi Film Lot, the team that was conducting these projects and I wanted to scout the film lot for potential shots. However, when we arrived, it was no longer open to tourists and no filming seemed to be taking place there. A no-nonsense, heavyweight security guard refused to let us in despite our team leader telling him which organization she represented. He said we needed to wait for his supervisor.

So we waited for about an hour until a black car finally rolled up to the Bayi Film Lot's main gate. The man driving the car opened his window and glanced over an application letter the team leader had prepared and gave her several suggestions on how to revise it. He then kindly let us in to the film lot to scout it out.

The team and I trudged through the mud (it had rained heavily the night before), and the other women were wearing delicate, thin-soled shoes, so it was quite an ordeal for them. I had a bit of an easier time because I was wearing sneakers I had borrowed from Jackie; after all, I already knew what to expect at Bayi, and the sneakers happened to be the kind Chinese soldiers wear, Jackie had told me. (As a foreign woman with relatively big feet for my short stature, I roughly have the same shoe size as Jackie, with my guessing Jackie has the average shoe size of a Chinese man, at local shoe size 41 or 42.) Interestingly, Jackie had told me that his father had massaged his feet so that they wouldn't grow too wide and remain relatively slim; the reason behind this was greater convenience in buying shoes in China.

But back to our story. The film lot remained more or less unchanged since my last visit with Jackie in 2015 — minus the action, of course. The plan was to do a Livestream program featuring a Chinese actor (Jackie) and a foreign actor and then do two mini-documentaries featuring each actor, with me as an add-on for the documentary about Jackie. The theme was the "Chinese Dream," a rather open concept that emerged in 2012 and is originally about making China a moderately prosperous society and a more advanced nation on different levels. The Chinese Dream concept lends itself well to various situations and personal interpretations and may include not only Chinese, but also foreigners. Similarly, the American Dream is traditionally about attaining one's own version of success by working hard but has been called into question by younger Americans. As for the Chinese Dream concept, well, let's wait and see how it develops.

Now our mini-documentary would be part of over a dozen Chinese-English bilingual Chinese Dream documentaries that the media organization would make as part of a series, documenting how foreigners from different countries and professions were living their dreams in China. I was lucky to piggyback on Jackie for this, and vice versa. We were billed as "cross-border lovers" and the episode had the rather flowery title "Chinese Dream, My Dream: Cross-border Lovers' Creative Life."

I was asked to help find a foreign actor to participate in the series, but it was hard to find someone who had several hours to spare on the September day we wanted to film from among Jackie's and my actor contacts. One of Jackie's contacts finally introduced me to George, an American actor from Chicago who had played Edgar Snow in a Chinese TV series.

We brought our own costumes and makeup, and I also brought some snacks and water because we were far away from a venue where we could get a hot lunch. Jackie dressed in a dark blue Chinese men's robe called a *changpao* (worn during the Qing dynasty and for some decades afterwards) as well as cloth shoes. Maoling (茂伶), who was the anchor for the Livestream, wore a blouse that she said was typically worn by female teachers during the Republic of China period (1912-1949), before the founding of the People's Republic. I wore a Chinese-style top that was light blue and matched the blues Maoling and Jackie were wearing, as well as the gray stones of the fortress at the Bayi Film Lot, so the color scheme was pretty cool in the smoldering September heat. As in a movie, these little details should be taken into consideration to achieve a better overall effect.

TAMMY TREICHEL

Jackie and I as well as the media team arrived together at the Bayi Film Lot, and George arrived shortly later. He emerged from his taxi holding a Starbucks coffee cup and looking very self-assured. He came in the exact same suit he had worn for his work as Edgar Snow, and he even showed us the sweat stains from his acting days on his collar.

The announcement for the Livestream read in a telegraph-like manner: "Live Coming Up: Join us at 0600 GMT to meet Jackie Chan's stand-in & see how Edgar Snow dressed in 1930s Beijing at a war movie film lot." Whereas the Livestream, as the word suggests, would be broadcast live, the mini-documentaries, each two to three minutes long, would be released later after editing.

Maoling, a true professional, was very well prepared and tried her best to give both George and Jackie a fair amount of air time during our Livestream, which was not an easy feat. George was shorter than Jackie and had violet blue-colored eyes. He had been in China for a decade and used his excellent Chinese for his acting work; he wowed us with his eloquence and industry knowledge.

During the interview, George called acting storytelling, an activity, he said, that human beings have been engaging in since the beginning of language. What makes acting valuable, he believed, is that we are telling good, meaningful stories to the people who are watching.

While George, Jackie and I were busy trying to share our Chinese Dreams with the world, the mosquitoes at the Bayi Film Lot proved to be very aggressive, and threatened to turn our Chinese Dreams into veritable nightmares. The media team members later posted mosquito selfies on WeChat showing the angry-looking welts on their arms and legs, but we persevered.

The "Chinese Dream" documentary featuring Jackie and me turned out to be a success with over one million views. They did a wonderful job creating it, and a British man I knew described the finished product as "charming." A young Chinese coworker described it as "so sweet" and the relationship Jackie and I enjoy as an example of "true love" that "inspires" him in his own quest for Mrs. Right.

When I look at some photos we took on that day, next to the group photos, my favorite ones are those of Jackie shaking hands with George and the team winding its way up Bayi's steep fortress, carefully climbing over rubble, with George gallantly helping Maoling up in her high heels. I think it captures the spirit of the day quite well—a project involving people from East and West helping each other in a spirit of good will with a common objective, despite the heavy mud and mosquitoes and together overcoming some minor misunderstandings and challenges.

The young woman from the team who gave me the shooting plan wrote me that she had heard that Jackie and I are a "lovey-dovey" couple, and the plan did call for several romantic shots that were later used in the mini-documentary. Next to my powdering my nose and Jackie doing a kung fu-like move with a fan, the documentary showed Jackie and me marveling at a cigarette ad featuring a pirate, going over a film script Jackie had once actually used, and my brushing his thick, gorgeous hair and buttoning his robe.

There was an ethereal glow behind me, somewhat of a "halo" that the camera caught when Jackie and I went over the film script. The lighting was superb; after all, lighting is perhaps the most important part when filming something. In another shot, Jackie gently touches my hair, a detail I had initially missed but the camera can pick up subtleties that our consciousness is not tuned into. In the last shot, Jackie and I walked hand-in-hand towards the fortress. We had no problem obliging with the content of the shots; we did not even have to "act" because we are naturally affectionate and, of course, the real thing. One Chinese member of the team who posted the video to her WeChat account after it was released joked, "狗粮来了！" ("Here comes some PDA!")

In the mini-documentary, I introduce Jackie and myself and briefly say why I enjoy being with him. "I really like his outgoing personality, his optimism, his can-do attitude and also his appreciation for small gestures. I think that is very rare in today's world," I said. After all, many people today are so rushed or don't have the awareness or upbringing to say "thank you," so if someone actually does show his or her appreciation that scores them points with me. Remember when I mentioned previously how Jackie had thanked me for giving him a home?

I also touched upon how I help Jackie with his acting work by going over his scripts and about my own acting stint as Joan Hinton, whom I described as being "very much committed to peace and to the development of the human race." With the camera rolling, I then chuckled when casually mentioning how during that stint "I had to ride a horse and I also had to wrestle with an Inner Mongolian lady, so it was quite an experience." Indeed, as I said in the "Chinese Dream" documentary, I have discovered more aspects of myself since coming to China.

Jackie, too, picked up on this during the interview and said, "Although she is a foreigner, I feel she is more like a Chinese," but I think the best way of describing myself at this point would be a foreigner with some Chinese characteristics. A coworker has also remarked that I act quite a bit like a "typical" Chinese woman, being rather "quiet" and "sweet," although I do have my "typical foreigner" moments as well here in Beijing, as I can be quite candid.

However, if I was in danger of causing discomfort to the Chinese I was interacting with, Jackie would dismiss my behavior for their benefit as "foreigners are in the habit of doing this or that," words which appeared to soothe them immediately.

There was a bit of comic relief in the already light-hearted video when Jackie caught me unawares during the interview and asked me in Chinese, "What would you like to have for dinner?" I spontaneously and truthfully replied "dumplings" in Chinese because "I like dumplings, I'd like to eat dumplings every day." I suppose I should have elaborated and said I like to eat Jackie's home-made dumplings.

At the end of the mini-documentary, I borrow a quick quote from Jack Dawson in the blockbuster movie *Titanic* by talking about the importance of seizing the day ("making each day count") and by extension, not taking life, the people and the opportunities it brings, for granted. For sure, it may sound trite to many, but life has taken on a new meaning for me after my father's passing away at age 75 after a devastating illness. That seminal event forced me to suddenly take stock of my own life with all the twists and turns I had experienced, make some sense out of my adventures and misadventures in Beijing and determine what I wanted to make out of life's package deal for me.

In fact, James Cameron's *Titanic* movie that came out in 1997 wasn't as bad as I had originally thought; when it first hit the movie screens, I didn't even watch it. I initially dismissed it as more Hollywood cheese, but after seeing it only several years after its debut, I realized it does have its merits—a good love story between an upper-class woman (Rose) and an American migrant worker (Jack), lots of action, reasonably good acting and some nuggets of wisdom as far as Hollywood is capable of them, e.g., Rose muses that a woman's heart is a "deep ocean of secrets" (however, I suppose I have worn my heart on my sleeve here). But I have digressed. Back to Tammy, the American expat, and Jackie, the former Chinese migrant worker, in Beijing.

TAMMY TREICHEL

As Confucius said, at age forty, you have no more doubts or illusions; to put it bluntly, I was running out of time for tolerating BS in my life. Continuing to run an exhausting rat race and trying to keep up with the Joneses are not my life's goal. I have come to Beijing to seek an alternative lifestyle for this stage in my life—not quite unlike Henry David Thoreau's going to the woods in *Walden* because he wanted to lead a spiritually richer, more intense, and perhaps what one could call more of a barebones existence. Yes, you could say that Beijing has, to some extent, been my Walden Pond and woods and the hutong house my cabin.

My aim is to lead a life that makes sense to me, as an ordinary person, on a small scale, and enriching it with creative projects together with a person I love—Jackie. Life as such has no meaning, it is up to us individually to endow it with meaning. So my personal manifesto is to surround yourself with people you love, engage in activities you enjoy and find a place where you feel at home.

"I just have a very simple personal dream and that is leading a meaningful life every day, making the most of every day, making every day count, doing something creative with my Chinese or foreign friends here in Beijing and enjoying each day," I said in the mini-documentary. "Because life is short, and you don't know what life will bring."

Despite the ups and downs that life has brought and is certain to bring, I told a Chinese friend that I had found my "happy ending" with Jackie.

"Happy ending?" she asked, incredulously. No, that sounded too good to be true, too much like a fairytale ending in today's cold and brutal world!

I suppose instead I should have said, "Happy continuation of my life with Jackie in China."

HUTONG HEARTTHROBS

Epilogue

Jackie and Tammy eloped to Xi'an on September 21, 2020, the International Day of Peace.

"What a scamp!" my sister Heidi allegedly told my mother after she heard of our elopement. Both were pleased by the news, as was Jackie's family. "We are very happy," Jackie's mother told us after Jackie had informed her. "Now you have great responsibility," was Jackie's father's reaction.

No, there wasn't a romantic beachside proposal at sunset. There wasn't a dinner with iced champagne in a fancy restaurant and Jackie having me fish a fat diamond ring out of a dessert (bad idea, folks, when you think of the choking hazard). There was no serenading or dropping to one knee. In 2020, there was only Covid-19 and a looming sense of crisis—and a shared understanding between Jackie and myself that we would ride out this and ensuing challenges together as man and wife. Next to the romantic sentiment there was also a practical component; we didn't want to be separated and a marriage license would be a better guarantee that we could stay together and have a shared future.

Jackie did some research on how we could get legally married in China. Matters were a bit more complicated as he was marrying a foreigner (to date, China allows a foreigner to get married to a Chinese citizen in China whereas registering marriages between two foreigners isn't possible in China any longer). Moreover, he wasn't a Beijing resident. As a *beipiao*, that meant he had to take me to his home province, Shaanxi, to get married. But because he was marrying a foreigner, the certificate couldn't be issued in his hometown; we had to go to Shaanxi's provincial capital, Xi'an, to get it. This was a blessing in disguise as it was nearly impossible to return to Jackie's hometown at that time due to local Covid restrictions and strict quarantine requirements; traveling to Xi'an from Beijing and back would require no quarantine, just scanning health codes to board trains and enter public venues.

We contacted the marriage registration office in Xi'an well in advance to learn what documents they required. There were some hiccups because Jackie no longer had his original military discharge papers (they had been stolen in Beijing) and only a photo copy, but we found a way around it; his discharge information must have been on record. Chinese who are in the military are prohibited from marrying foreigners, so proof of the discharge was vital.

For my part, among other documents, I needed a marriageability affidavit from the US Embassy in Beijing, which I then needed to have translated into Chinese and notarized. The translator made a mistake and had listed my current status as "widowed" and thus eligible to wed; thankfully, I caught the error and had it corrected before we electronically submitted the documents to Xi'an and specified the date we wanted to register our marriage, September 21, 2020. I remember losing a bit of sleep due to worrying about our documents, whereas happy-go-lucky Jackie slept as soundly as ever.

This was real life; it surely wasn't as simple as in the movies, where you can just defy the establishment and waltz into a church or marriage registrar's office and ask to be wed. No, marriages are rarely conducted on the spot; you have to prepare well in advance and make sure your paperwork is complete and beyond reproach.

The marriage registration office of the municipal civil affairs bureau in Xi'an informed us that our documents had been accepted and that we could come on September 21 to get legally married. I had suggested the date to Jackie because of its symbolic significance, the International Day of Peace, and Jackie wholeheartedly agreed. Yet Jackie and I were still cautious and didn't want to inform our families; best do it after the fact. After all, with the ever-changing Covid situation at the time, you never knew which way the wind was blowing, plus, if you are dealing with bureaucrats, you might run into red tape.

To my delight, I found a nice hotel not too far from the marriage registration office and I got us a good deal because there weren't too many travelers at that time. Jackie and I took the high-speed train directly from Beijing to Xi'an for several hours, checked into our hotel, and woke up on September 21 with a sense of anticipation and purpose.

It was raining rather heavily that day, but our mood wasn't dampened in the least. Jackie bought me a large bouquet of red roses and white lilies as a surprise before we went to register our marriage in the afternoon. "It's what I should do," he said simply and smiled sweetly. I looked deep into his brownie-colored eyes. I felt so loved and warm despite the cold rain outside. Interestingly, folklore has it that rain on your wedding day brings good luck, one reason being that the rain represents renewal and the washing away of old.

We were greeted by the woman at the marriage registration office. She was the only person present; most of the time we were wearing masks and conducted our conversation through a thick pane of glass due to Covid. The registrar handled our original documents wearing white gloves and then sat us down and explained the legal implications of marriage to us, asked us if we knew about any preexisting health conditions our partner had, and similar matters. Jackie and I felt like schoolchildren, seated on a school bench and being lectured to by our teacher. We felt very shy; well prepared and yet totally unprepared. Then we signed the paperwork and the woman issued us two marriage certificates that looked like little booklets with red covers that contained a photo of both of us inside, one for each party.

"Your documents are in the system. If there are any objections from the US side, I'll phone you within the next twenty-four hours," she told us. "Otherwise, congratulations!" Well, I suppose they wanted to ensure I wasn't a bigamist and already had a husband stashed away somewhere... there were no objections; no call came. If there had been, I wonder what they would have done with our issued marriage certificates.

We took some photos posing with our marriage booklets in the marriage registration office, and another couple who had come to register their marriage offered to help with our photos, but the lighting was too poor. I was wearing a qipao and Jackie a suit with different kinds of buttons on the sleeves and a colorful checkered tie that I had once bought for him in the US. Of course, he had thought long and hard about what he wanted to wear on his official wedding day. We clasped hands as we walked out of the marriage registration office into the heavy autumn rain, ducking under our umbrellas and tightly holding on to each other.

Back at the hotel, Jackie closed and bolted the door of our room. My heart started beating fast. He pulled me close, closer... and whipped out a selfie stick. It was time for a Kodak moment with our marriage booklets because the lighting was better here; Jackie was being a stickler for the perfect elopement selfie.

After phoning Jackie's parents to tell them the good news, we went to a restaurant for some hearty Xi'an noodle dishes and beer. We then spent a week in Xi'an exploring the city in detail, renting bikes to ride around the city wall, strolled around the Muslim quarter, and climbed to the top of nearby Mount Cuihua, which had a moderately high altitude of just under two thousand meters.

The misty mountaintop with its old pine trees looked as if it had been lifted out of a Chinese ink wash painting. Jackie taught me the hack of carrying my purse on a strong stick over my shoulder as we wound our way up the mountain, up, up, up. Once we reached the mountaintop, a new world was at our feet. The view was breathtaking; we were floating on a sea of rag-sized clouds.

We also enjoyed other local marvels before returning to Beijing. It was only then that I dropped the bombshell news to my mother and sister.

It had been my secret fantasy to have a ceremony in a tiny wedding chapel located on the historic Generals Highway in Annapolis, Maryland, where my mother had a vacation home, or perhaps in an Elvis Presley-themed wedding chapel somewhere, maybe even Las Vegas, with an Elvis Presley impersonator crooning "Can't Help Falling In Love" and me wearing a frilly white dress. I wished for something relatively remote, romantic, a touch tacky and intimate, with only Jackie and myself and perhaps close family members present.

Jackie for his part was partial to a large glitz-and-glamor wedding in a hotel, with a catwalk for bride and groom and an MC, elaborate flower arrangements and wedding candy bags for the guests, typical Chinese-style, with his countless Yang County relatives present. So far, we haven't realized these two fantasies but we can always hold a belated wedding party once the time is right, and maybe combine elements of these two fantasies, why not? We have, however, taken some wedding photos at a photo studio in Beijing, as is customary in China, and we even poached one of their photographers to do a separate wedding photo shoot in our hutong neighborhood.

So if you are looking for a climax, the only thing I can point you to is a sense that after having spent several happy years together as boyfriend and girlfriend, Jackie and I could and would also overcome difficulties together as a married couple. After all, marriage is for better or for worse, and many people tend to ignore the "for worse" part until it actually comes. And that it surely will. If you can survive "for worse" together, rest assured that you can also survive "for better"!

Acknowledgments

Special thanks goes to my publisher, Graham Earnshaw, for being supportive of this project from the start, his sharp criticism, dark sense of humor and encouragement to produce my best, my editor Victoria Graham for her patience and professionalism — she really understood what I was trying to say and had the magic to pull it out of me. My appreciation also goes to Guo Fengqing (郭丰庆), for helping me with translations of Jackie's life story after Jackie had dictated his experiences to me and Walter Fung, editor of the Society for Anglo-Chinese Understanding's (SACU) magazine *China Eye*, who kindly let me reproduce some material I had written for them. The same applies to *HaiVision* magazine as well as *Beijing Review*. I am also grateful to Lily Chen, publisher of *Asian Fortune*, who gave me permission to republish my "Rubbing Shoulders with Jackie Chan" episode here. Finally, I consider myself fortunate to enjoy the unconditional support and love of my family East and West.

Afterword
By Andrew Hicks, author of
Jack Jones: A True Friend to China

This book has some beautiful themes that are close to my heart, about the thrill and stimulus of living in a foreign country far from home and of falling in love with someone of a different culture. Succeeding in a long-term relationship and marriage is always a mountain to climb, but it is even more so when trying to understand your partner across the barriers of culture and language. Yet equally, such relationships are especially rewarding as this is the best way to feel at home in and learn about your adoptive home country.

Such individuals courageous enough to marry across cultures have to be adventurers, as indeed is the American author of this delightful book. She tells us the story of her American mother marrying her German father, of herself studying at a top university in Germany and ultimately of working in China and falling for its people and culture. And, of course, for her Chinese boyfriend whose life as an actor has likewise been unorthodox and exciting.

The couple faces many challenges: the death of the author's father, long separations and dealing with the many issues of reconciling dramatically different upbringings. But what comes across very strongly is the sheer joy of living in so rich and different a culture, all the intricacies of daily life being vividly described and evoked. And the book suggests the positive conclusion that we can be drawn together by our common humanity rather than divided by our differences.

I also associate with the author's achievement in writing of young lives with much verve and detail that draws the reader in so powerfully. I too have constructed such a story, a novel called *Thai Girl*, about how a young Englishman is totally perplexed by the reactions of the young Thai woman he is wooing with great passion but not always successfully. Writing a book is a mountain to climb, but a belief in the importance of its themes is fundamental to its success.

The other common aspect that I too have written about is how, despite all the tensions and mutual suspicion between powerful countries the role that individuals can play in breaking down barriers is of great significance. In Chapter 3, the author tells how we met in Beijing and discussed my recent book, *Jack Jones: A True Friend to China*. This relates how through the turbulent years of the 1940s, several hundred mainly British and American volunteers distributed medical supplies over the ravaged roads of China and provided aid and doctors to people in great need. These volunteers were conscientious objectors who were excused from military service, allowed to pursue their principles of giving humanitarian aid without strings attached and served as ambassadors striving for better international understanding.

In fact, like them, we are all ambassadors when we travel abroad and in particular when we settle in a foreign country and make it our own. Seen in this light, the romantic adventure in this book of Tamara and Jackie is a heroic and heart-warming one that I applaud. For the Western reader, we share Tamara's constant curiosity to learn more about China and we learn much along with her. And the Chinese reader will discover how an American perceives and respects their own great country and how she adapts to living there.

All the personal minutiae of a shared life in China make for fascinating reading but the book has a greater significance as an inspiring example of how individuals can transcend the negative aspects of centuries of tensions between their countries and provide a microcosm of how things ought to be between us. I, too, love China and its culture and I commend this book as a fine example of what can and should be aspired to both in personal and international relations. The human predicament is universal and we are always more similar than different.

Andrew Hicks, former senior lecturer in Law at the University of Hong Kong and author of *Thai Girl*, *My Thai Girl and I*, and *Jack Jones: A True Friend to China*

Hampshire, UK
January 2024

About The Author

Tammy (Tamara) Arehart Treichel is an American with a passion for two things: China and writing. After graduating with an award-winning PhD in English on Herman Melville's *Moby-Dick*, she worked as a freelancer for various China-related publications. Born in Washington, D.C., she found a second lease on life and true love in China, where she has lived for over a decade and is working as an English editor at a local news agency in Beijing. Tammy greatly enjoys exploring all things China with her Chinese man, a former security guard-turned-actor named Jackie. They live in an old hutong (alleyway) house in a historic part of Beijing together with three rescue cats and numerous house lizards.